FOOD AND BEVERAGE
MANAGEMENT AND COST CONTROL

Jay Prakash Kant

AMAN PUBLICATIONS
NEW DELHI

Published by
Rajiv Jain for Aman Publications
LG-4A, Ganpati Bhawan,
4675-B/21, Ansari Road,
Darya Ganj, Delhi-110002
E-mail: sshjbs@yahoo.com

2015

Reprint 2018

Food and Beverage: Management and Cost Control

ISBN–978-81-8204-089-2

SOLE DISTRIBUTOR
JINDAL BOOK SERVICES
LG-4A, Ganpati Bhawan,
4675-B/21, Ansari Road,
Darya Ganj, Delhi-110002

Jacket Designed by :
S.M. Graphics

Printed by:
Balaji Offest, Delhi, India

FOOD AND BEVERAGE

MANAGEMENT AND COST CONTROL

FOREWORD

It gives me immense pleasure to congratulate Mr. Jay Prakash Kant, Faculty at Chandigarh Institute of Hotel Management for his work titled "Food and Beverage: Management and Cost Control" in which he has given his valuable inputs.

The book is worth appraising too with all the topics combined and arranged accordingly to NCMHCT syllabus and guidelines for Food and Beverage: Management and Cost Controls.

The book is complete in all aspects with each point diagrammatically explained with use of references, examples, questionnaires and glossary which adds up to salient features of this book. I take this opportunity to recommend the volume for the students of hospitality education.

I would like to convey my best wishes to Mr. Jay Prakash Kant for his work and hope this book emerges as a most sought after reference book.

(Tej Krishan Razdan)
Principal/Secretary
Chandigarh Institute of Hotel Management
& Catering Technology
Sector 42-D, Chandigarh

राष्ट्रीय होटल प्रबन्ध एवं केटरिंग तकनालॉजी परिषद
(पर्यटन मंत्रालय, भारत सरकार)
NATIONAL COUNCIL FOR HOTEL MANAGEMENT AND CATERING TECHNOLOGY
(Ministry of Tourism, Govt. of India)
ए-34, सेक्टर 62, नोएडा - 201309 उत्तर प्रदेश))
A-34, Sector 62, NOIDA - 201309 (Uttar Pradesh)
टैलि/Tel: 0120-2590600-623 टैलिफैक्स/Telefax : 0120-2402819/2402820
ईमेल-/e-mail : www.nchmctadmn@gmail.com वेबसाईट/Website: www.nchm.nic.in

NCHMCT

अतुल्य भारत
Incredible!ndia

FOREWORD

I take this opportunity to congratulate Mr. Jay Prakash Kant, Faculty at Chandigarh Institute of Hotel Management for his precious efforts on volume "Food and Beverage Management and Cost control" in which he has given his valuable inputs.

The book is worth appraising too since it meets the NCMHCT syllabus and guidelines for Food and Beverage: Management and Cost Controls. The book explained the topics with use of references, examples, questionnaires and glossary.

I would like to convey my best wishes to Mr. Jay Prakash Kant for his work.

27.1.15

L. K. Ganguli

Director (A & F) & Member Secretary

And I/c Director (S)

National Council for Hotel Management & Catering Technology

A 34, Sector 62, NOIDA.

FOREWORD

A desirable development in India, in recent years, has been the widespread application of science and technology to problems in the fields of Food and Beverage and Cost Control. Better methods of cost control can help to increase the profit and effective availability of our food resources. Hotel Management Institutes are gaining popularity and the growing numbers of colleges in this field is an attribute to the demand and performance in the field.

It is pleasure to acknowledge the efforts of Mr. Jay Prakash Kant, Faculty Chandigarh Institute of Hotel Management & Catering Technology who has taken the initiative in the field of Cost Control Management and has made an attempt to introduce better ideas in this field. The book has covered all the topics from the syllabus prescribed by National Council for Hotel Management and Catering Technology, Noida in the topic of Food and Beverage Service and Cost Control.

I hope that this book will reach and provide valuable information to the students of Hotel Management.

Dehradun
3rd November 2014

Mukul Dimri
Principal Incharge
IHM Dehradun

AROMA
SINCE 1953

Man Mohan S Kohli

Member Executive Committee :
Federation of Hotel & Restaurant Associations of India (2001-03)
Hotel & Restaurant Association of Northern India ((1990-2003)
CEO, Aroma Group of Hospitality Establishments

FOREWORD

In present times and more so in times to come, controlling the cost of FOOD AND BEVERAGE shall remain a major challenge. The work **"FOOD & BEVERAGE SERVICE: MANAGEMENT AND COST CONTROL"** by Mr. Jay Prakash Kant addressing the costing factor is indeed an indispensable handbook. It is said that good food is not just good taste but also the cost. The young students, chefs and the hospitality professionals, all alike, shall find Mr. Kant's book a reference, a guide and in many ways an omnipresent mentor.

I sincerely hope, rather `am confident that this book will adorn every hospitality professional's bookshelf.

Man Mohan S Kohli

THE AROMA
Business Hotel
0172-2700051, 4010000, 9855-568-855, E-mail: mail@hotelaroma.com, Web: www.hotelaroma.com
AQUAMARINE
Boutique Hotel
0172-5014000, 5047800, E-Mail: info@hotelaquamarine.com, Web: www.hotelaquamarine.com
Himalaya Marg, Sector 22-C, Chandigarh-160022, India

ACKNOWLEDGMENT

I would like to mention certain people and organizations who have either directly or indirectly contributed towards this book.

First and Foremost, I would like to mention **Mr. T.K. Razdan** honorable Principal **Chandigarh Institute of Hotel Management and Catering Technology, CIHMCT, Chandigarh** for having his fidelity in me and constantly providing me with his guidance and support in writing this book.

Also heartiest thanks to **Mr. Ravi Prakash** honorable Principal, **Delhi Institute of Hotel Management,** Delhi who was my mentor and discovered a teacher in me as Principal at **Institute of Hotel Management,** Dehradun and still continues to inspire me to the present day.

I would like to thank my learning and educating institution of **IHM,** Meerut, from where I have learnt and went on to grow as a professional.

I am grateful to professionals in the industry and academics who have in some ways influenced the development of this book.

Last but not the least; I would like to thank my parents **Shri A.P. Kant** and **Smt. Rajwati Kant** for their unconditional support to make me empowered and given me education and made me worthwhile to write a book which would benefit many, my wife **Saroj Prakash Kant** who has given her fullest support in this venture of mine and shown immense patience while I sat late nights to compile this work and my children **Pihu & Priyan**, the fortune of my life who have been a great support and cheered me up on every instance and added humor in moments of fragile stress.

My sincere thanks to **Aman Publications** who have given me their valuable time and have considered my capable efforts to help me provide the platform for my book to publish and distribute under their esteemed and famed label.

I would also like to thank my students at **CIHMCT,** Chandigarh specially **Siddharth Mittal** with a great sense of gratitude for being the primary inspiration in compilation of this book, and for their valuable inputs at various stages of my learning and development.

Jay Prakash Kant

PREFACE

"Beware of Small Expenses. A small leak will sink a great ship."
Benjamin Franklin

"Money should be mastered, not served"
Syrus, Maxims

"There are people who have money and people who are rich"
Coco Chanel

Funds, Wealth, Treasure, Lucre or in simple words 'Money' has become an important crave and exigency of an individuals' life. Every aspect of a good business and life now depends upon the Profits and losses, earned and degraded by responsible personnel.

A very famous Idiom by Benjamin Franklin quoted as "A penny saved is a penny earned." Stresses upon the importance of methods about savings and expenditure control which I have tried to speak and implement through this book. I wish and hope with this book student may learn study and become better managers of their life and Job. Through this book I have endeavored the prime of my efforts to inkling and acknowledge the reader to the notions and concepts of cost controlling easily and effectively, this book has been compiled after a thorough research of market and yielding industry.

Being first the of its kind this book complies studies according to the syllabus of 'Food and Beverage Cost Control' & 'Food and Beverage Management' provided by **National Council of Hotel Management and Catering Technology (NCHMCT)**, with the study material strictly foot held upon **NCHMCT** curriculum I hope to find it's appointment in many other professional courses too.

This book covers wide aspects and pro et contra of the concerned subjects, and probably falls on the plot rightly.

And finally through the columns of this book I, Jay Prakash Kant would dote on to educate and empower the students and future professionals with the most powerful tools of **Knowledge & Management**.

CONTENTS

	Foreword by Tej Krishan Razdan	*(v)*
	Foreword by L.K. Ganguli	*(vi)*
	Foreword by Mukul Dimri	*(vii)*
	Foreword by Man Mohan S. Kohli	*(viii)*
	Acknowledgment	*(ix)*
	Preface	*(xi)*
Unit 1	Food Cost Control	1
Unit 2	Food Control Cycle	13
Unit 3	Receiving Control	38
Unit 4	Storing and Issuing Control	64
Unit 5	Production Control	86
Unit 6	Sales Control	94
Unit 7	Cost Dynamics	114
Unit 8	Sales Concept	122
Unit 9	Inventory Control	127
Unit 10	Beverage Control	139
Unit 11	Sales Control (Management)	150
Unit 12	Budgetary Control	159
Unit 13	Variance Analysis	165
Unit 14	Breakeven Analysis	171
Unit 15	Menu Merchandising	178
Unit 16	Menu Engineering	188
Unit 17	Management Information Services (MIS)	192
	Glossary	203

UNIT 1

FOOD COST CONTROL

INTRODUCTION TO COST CONTROL

COST

Cost is generally defined as reduction in the value of assets for the purpose of securing benefits or gains in the food beverage business; cost means the price to the hotel or restaurants of goods and services when the good are consumed or the services rendered.

COSTING

Costing may be defined as the technique and process of ascertaining costs. Costing means simply the process of arithmetic, means of memorandum statements or the methods of integral control.

The cost of any item may be expressed in a variety of ways such as:

- Units of weight
- Unit of volume
- Total per individual portion

For example, the cost of liquor can be expressed in terms of the cost per bottle, per drink, or per ounce.

The following are the methods of costing:

1. *Batch costing:* The identification and assignment of costs related to producing a set amount of goods. This includes all fixed and variable cost for producing the batch.
2. *Job costing:* It involves the calculation of costs involved in a construction "job" or the manufacturing of goods done in discrete batches.

3. *Contract costing:* Contract Costing is a special type of job costing where the unit of cost is a single contract. Contract itself is a cost centre and is executed under the customer's specifications.
4. *Operation costing and process costing:* Process costing is an accounting methodology that traces and accumulates direct costs and allocates indirect costs of a manufacturing process. Costs are assigned to products, usually in a large batch, which might include an entire month's production.
5. *Unit, output and operating costing:* In finance, unit cost is the cost of a single no. product and output cost is the cost required to produce a good output and operating cost is the cost to carry on operations well.
6. *Marginal costing:* In finance, marginal cost is the change in the total cost that arises when the quantity produced has an increment by unit. That is, it is the cost of producing one more unit of a good. In general terms, marginal cost at each level of production includes any additional costs required to produce the next unit.
7. *Food and beverage sales:* Food & Beverage cost are an important activity in the hotel industry. It deals with the techniques to setup and maintain total cost control systems which can help have to earn profits in the business.

CONCEPT OF COSTING

1. To know cost
2. To fix the selling price
3. Cost controlling
4. Preparation of profit and loss account and balance sheet
5. Operating policies of the organization

ADVANTAGES OF COSTING

1. Helps in proper planning of the food & beverage operations
2. Keeps a check over the accuracy of financial accounts
3. Helps in establishing the prices of menu, dishes & beverages
4. Helps in comparing cost per unit of a specific period or two or more periods of time
5. Somewhat specifies how the hotel is into profit or loss
6. Helps in proper understanding of the quality and packaging of materials or goods
7. Develops an effective costing system and controls the cost too
8. Helps in making closing stock value sheet

COST CONTROL

It can be defined as keeping of various costs by the management in line with standards according to the control policy of the hotel. Cost control starts with the setting up of business, profit and financial objectives.

Cost control is achieved by financial as well as intentional control over budgeting which is generally concerned with the points given below:

1. Setting up of proper standards
2. Monitoring input and output i.e. actual performance
3. Identifying of actual variance by preparing cost groups graph (given after types of costs).
4. Take corrective measures and actions in order to have a control over cost and achieve maximum profits.

APPROACH TO COST CONTROL

1. Pre-Operational Control – such control is exercised in various areas before the actual operation and is more useful in those areas where volume & sales both can be forecasted with a high degree of certainty.
2. Post-operational Control – in this type of control, standards and objectives are presented before the employee of the organisation and operations are then performed according to their standards and the S.O.P.'s

OBJECTIVES & ADVANTAGES OF COST CONTROL

1. To establish S.O.P.'s
2. Fixing menu price and quotations of special events
3. To prevent wastage of raw material, time, labour etc.
4. To avoid frauds by staff or clients
5. To prepare and submit accurate management report sheets
6. To take corrective remedial measures and actions for improvement and welfare
7. Proper analysis of points of sales
8. Cost analysis of food and beverage material being purchased
9. Calculation of gross profit
10. Calculation of net profit
11. Establishing standard
12. Establishing procedure
13. Setting examples

14. Correcting and observing employees actions
15. Records and reports
16. Preparing and following budgets
17. Censoring and disciplining employees
18. Preparation of profit and loss account and balance sheet
19. Helps to know the market value of closing stock
20. Helps in proper fixing up of the selling prices of the F&B material

COST CONTROL IN FOOD & BEVERAGE OPERATIONS AND DEPARTMENT

Food & Beverage cost control is an important activity in the hotel industry. It deals with the techniques to setup and maintain total cost control systems which can help have to earn profits in the business.

The food and beverage in specific and hotel industry in general, lends itself to control because it is an instant business, and all the items sold are countable. All the items handled in the hotel and restaurants are portable and consumable by the staff. Therefore, by maintaining and analysing the food and beverage business, the responsible manager good early monitor and analyse the business and weak links can be identified and like ages stopped.

The costing of a product is very important in order to ascertain that what should be the selling price so that hoteliers can make a reasonable profit after meeting the cost of the product.

SALES

Generally sales are defined as an inflow of assets occurring as a result of going business. A sale is referred as the restaurants exchange of products or services for value, in the hotel industry. The value may be in cash or a promise to pay in cash. These sales are expressed in monitory terms for the value of goods and services.

SALES IN TERMS OF COST CONTROL

Sales expressed in terms of the quantity of units sold are very useful fir purpose of control. A restaurant may express sales per waiter in order to know the efficiency of service personnel and provide a basis of scheduling control. Sales of a restaurant could be expressed in terms of rupees or in numbers of persons served. All the food and beverage outlets try to increase sales in order that the profits may be maintained or increased. Management set the selling price of the product or services to be provided. The selling price is mainly determined on the basis of cost.

Control may be defend as a process by means of which manager tries to direct regulate and restrain the actions of people in order to achieve desired organizational goals with respect to financial success, promotion of better health, etc.

CONTROL TECHNIQUES

1. Establishing standards
2. Establishing procedures
3. Setting examples
4. Correcting and observing employees actions
5. Records and reports
6. Preparing and following budgets
7. Censuring and disciplining employees

1. ESTABLISHING STANDARDS

Standards can be defined as rules or measure establish for making comparison and judgement.

Quality standards are used for the degree of excellence of raw material and finished products. For example, meat is available in a number of trades and it is important to establish which grade will be used in preparation of menu items.

Quantity standards refer to measures of weight or count or volume. For example, an order of soup should be identified as to size of bowl or cup to be used. In beverages, a standard for liquors to be used is established by management in the preparation of particular drink.

A standard cost is an agreed upon cost of goods and services used to measure other costs.

2. ESTABLISHING PROCEDURES

Procedures are the methods or steps to be followed while preparing a product or performing jobs.

Standard procedure are the instructional steps or the correct methods and techniques for day to day operation of food and beverage business.

Ordering and purchase procedure are standardised to ensure that required quantity is acquired.

Receiving procedures are standardised to ensure that quality and quantity goods are received.

Storing and issuing procedures are standardised to ensure the safety against spoilage and theft.

3. SETTING EXAMPLES

The behaviour, actions, statements and attitude of the manager or leader influence the behaviour of individual employee.

Manager should conduct proper briefing of staff/employees.

A manager must be consistent in setting examples as well as directing, regulating and restraining examples and their actions.

4. CORRECTING AND OBSERVING EMPLOYEES ACTIONS

Actions of the employees must be observed by manager actions of the employees should be judged and corrected at appropriate time

Suppose a manager observes a bartender mixing two drinks without measuring ingredients and he fails to direct him to measure QUANTITIES as drinks are mixed. This will result that bartender could assume that such is acceptable and manager has missed an opportunity to control behaviour.

A manager should observe his employees actions to a great extent in hotels. In large hotels the managers observations cannot be direct. Therefore he may extract information from reports and records. These reports are like form of balance sheet, profit and loss account, income statement and ratios and more timely reports and records as daily, weekly, monthly.

5. PREPARING AND FOLLOWING BUDGETS

Realistic expression of business goals and objectives expressed in financial terms is called budget. It is a forecast of sales activity and an estimate of cost stated normally in rupees.

Large hotels establish overall financial budgets for the operations of entire business.

In a well established F & B operations these budgets are prepared with the help of historical information, anticipated changes, business environment, state policy, weather conditions and general economic etc.

6. CENSURING AND DISCIPLINING EMPLOYEE

The main objective of censuring and disciplining employees is to change or modify their job performances in order to control performance in such a way that job activity of each employee is consistent with the standards and procedure.

AIMS AND OBJECTIVES OF FOOD & BEVERAGES DEPARTMENT FOR CONTROLLING COST

1. The actions, statements and attitude of the leader influence the behaviour of individual employees
2. Manager should conduct proper briefing of staff/employees
3. Cost analysis of food and beverage material being purchased
4. Proper analysis of points of sales
5. To strictly follow the S.O.P.'s
6. To prepare and submit accurate management report sheet
7. To take corrective remedial measures and actions for improvement and welfare
8. To avoid frauds by staff/employee
9. To research more and more F&B products in market
10. To receive, handle & serve proper canned materials

BASIC AND FOOD COSTING

TYPES OF COSTS

1. **Fixed Cost** – these are those costs which have a very little relationship to the volume of business. As the volume of business increases or decreases these costs remain the same e.g. taxes, insurance, premiums, depreciation etc.

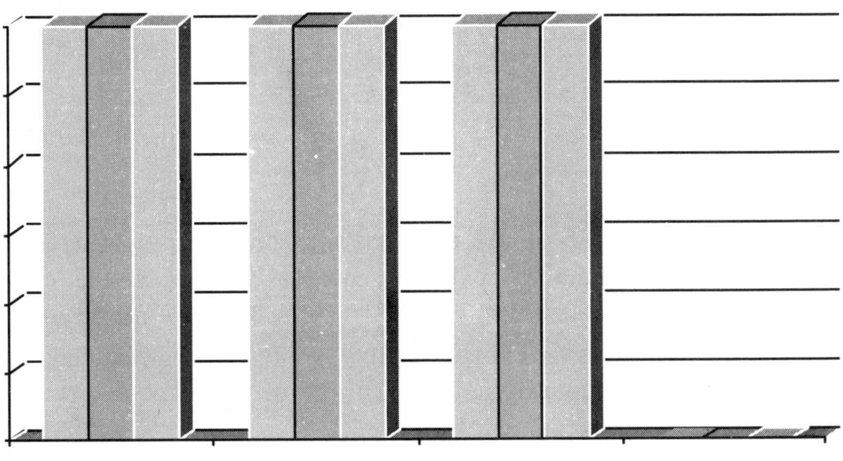

2. **Variable Cost**—these are those costs which are directly related to the volume of business, so every increase and decrease in cost e.g. food & beverage cost.

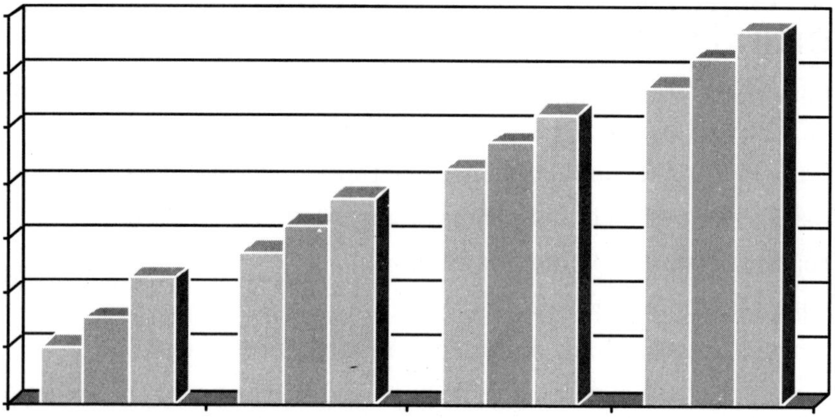

3. **Semi Variable/Semi Fixed Cost**—these costs vary with volume but not in direct proportion to it, e.g. cost of fuel, cost of cleaning material, replacement cost, telephone, laundry etc.

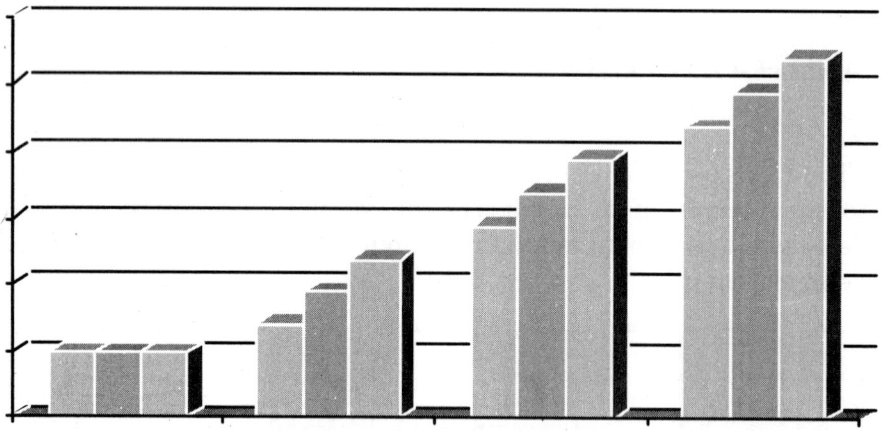

OTHER COSTS

1. Controllable Cost – These are those costs which can be changed without much difficulty. Variable costs are normally controllable costs, e.g. material cost.
2. Non-Controllable Cost – These are those costs that can be changed with great difficulty and usually not in a short run. Fixed costs are generally non-controllable, e.g. real estate taxes.

UNIT COST

It is the cost of a single unit of food or beverage portions as in cost of one steak or one martin.

ELEMENTS OF COST

1. Material Cost/Food cost
2. Labour Cost
3. Overhead cost

1. Material Cost: In material cost or food cost one has to take into account the opening stock, purchases and closing stock and the food consumed by staff or served as complimentary to guests usually spoilage of food is charged to the material cost.

TOTAL MATERIAL COST PERCENTAGE

= total material cost*100/total sale

To Control The Food Cost One Must Remember The Following Points:

a) Purchasing – The purchase department must ensure that the right quality of food is purchased at competitive price and right quantity of raw materials should be procured to keep a control over food cost.
b) Receiving and storing of raw material – the raw material received by stores must be inspected for the quantity, quality and specifications. All material received must be stored at proper place. No food item should get spoiled.
c) Issuing – All goods should be issued after a proper requisition, the store keeper must follow FIFO, LIFO according to their store policy.
d) Wastage & Spoilage – The wastage of portioning, storing, cooking should be as minimum as possible.
e) Proper Storing Of Cooked Food – In case of the cooked food is left at end of day then it must be stored at proper temperature and at proper place.
f) Ensure No Food Is Served Without bill – Incase the food is allowed to be picked up without proper bill, then this will increase the food cost.
g) Portion Control – The chef must ensure that dish is served as per the standard portion. A large portion will increase the food cost and a small portion will dissatisfy the guest.
h) Standard recipe – The chef must ensure that always standard recipe should be followed or otherwise the guest may not find the similar standard of dish and this will dissatisfy him/her.

2. Labour Cost: Apart from wages and salaries, all other expenses incurred of staff or on its welfare like medical re-imbursement, leave travel concession (L.T.C.), contribution towards the Employee's Provident Fund (E.P.F.), free food, uniform, accommodation, interest subsidy on loan, telephone bills etc.

TOTAL LABOURS COST PERCENTAGE

= total labour cost*100/total sale

Points to be considered in order to control labour cost:

1. The hotel must retain some of its staff as the new staff will take some time in adjusting till then they will give less output.
2. Most of the hotels tense money due to over staffing as it increases labour cost.
3. Over staffing does not improve quality of service.
4. Hotels must reduce overhead and other expenses on staff, like on accommodation, food, interest subsidy, L.T.C. etc.
5. If sale increase the labour cost percentage to sale will come down and vice versa
6. Hotel may stop any particular cuisine in any outlet if the cuisine is not doing well, to reduce the labour cost.

3. Overhead Cost: All other costs like office expenses, rent, interest, light and power, commission, water, gas, fuel, cooking coke and wood. Advertisement and marketing expenses, miscellaneous expenses, etc. are included under this head.

TOTAL OVERHEAD COST PERCENTAGE

= total overhead cost *100/total sale

Points to be considered to control overhead cost:

1. The hotel must study each and every cost deeply and in detail.
2. Hotel may consult the consultants.
3. The most common overhead cost is interest.
4. The debt should not be increased as it can become burden.
5. This debt can also lead to bank ruptcy.
6. The overhead cost should not affect the quality of goods/services as it can reduce sale.

BASIC & FOOD COST FORMULAS:

1. Total cost = total food cost + total labour cost + total Overhead cost
2. Net loss = total cost – total sale
3. Net profit = total sale – total cost
4. Gross profit = total sale – total food cost
5. Gross profit %age = gross profit * 100/total sale
6. Net loss %age = net loss * 100/ total sale
7. Net profit %age = net profit * 100/ total sale
8. Gross loss %age = gross loss * 100/ total sale
9. Food cost = total food cost / total sale
10. Beverage cost = total beverage cost / total sale
11. Food cost %age = food cost*100/total sale
12. Beverage cost %age= beverage cost*100/total sale

ILLUSTRATION

CALCULATE THE FOLLOWING

Cost percentage: when cost is rupees 400 and sale is rupees 1000

Cost: when cost percentage is 27% and sale is rupees 400

Sales: when cost percentage is 25% and cost is rupees 100

SOLUTION:

1. COST PERCENTAGE:

If rest 1000 is sales than cost is Rs 400
If rupee 1 is sale than is Rs 400/1000
If rupees 100 is sale than cost is 400*100/1000=40%

2. COST:

If rs 100 is sale than cost is Rs 27
If rupee 1 is sale than cost is 27/100
And if rs 400 is sale then cost is 27*400/100=108

3. SALES:

If rupee 25 is cost than sale is Rs 100

If rupee 1 is the cost than sale is 100/25

If rupee 100 is the cost than sale is 100*100/25=40

QUESTIONNAIRE

1. Define cost control. What are the objectives of cost control and explain in brief different types of cost?
2. Define variable, fixed, semi-variable costs in relation to catering industry?
3. Define the three elements of costs. Distinguish controllable cost with uncontrollable cost?
4. What do you understand by food cost control? Briefly explain the objectives and obstacles of food cost control?
5. How to control (I) food cost, (ii) labour cost, (iii) overhead cost?
6. Total sale of an institute canteen was Rs. 5, 000 and total cost was Rs. 6, 000.Find out the net loss and net loss percentage?

UNIT 2

FOOD CONTROL CYCLE

PURCHASING CONTROL

- Purchasing control is a function concern with search, selection, purchase, receipt, storage and final use of the commodity in accordance to the catering policy of the F&B department.
- The purchasing department's role is to make sure that supplies, equipment and services are available to the operation in quantities appropriate to predetermined standards, at the right price and at a minimum cost to meet desired standards.
- The person responsible for purchase of food and beverage is responsible for receiving, storage, and issuing will be involved with the purpose for which the item are purchased and final use of them.
- Generally, those responsible for purchasing have the authority to commit the establishment's funds to buying required goods or services.
- By following established purchasing procedures, an operation can avoid many purchasing pitfall such as panic buying, over or short purchasing, buying by price rather than by a combination of quality and price, pressure buying or what is probably quite common, satisfied buying.

PURCHASING CYCLE

See graph on next page 14.

AIMS OF PURCHASING POLICY

- The primary objective in purchasing of food is to obtain the best quality of materials based on specifications or standards established by the hotel, at the lowest possible price.

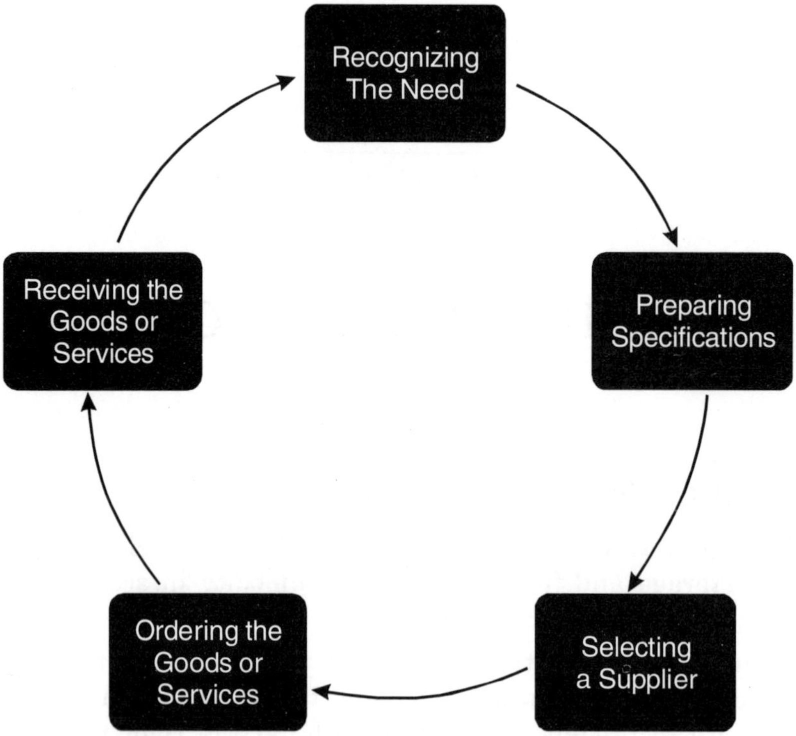

Purchasing Cycle

- Following effective buying methods and procedures.
- To establish a suitable buying standard for particular commodity for the hotel.
- Maintaining continuity in the respect of supply of materials to support the production schedule and the company's operations.
- Avoiding duplication, waste and obsolescence with respect to material.
- Maintaining standards in quality of materials, based on suitability for use.
- Doing above activities with the minimum investment consistent with safety and economic advantage.
- Developing good and reliable suppliers and ensuring satisfactory vendor relationships.
- Procuring materials at the lower cost consistent with quality.
- Maintaining company's competitive position by controlling costs relating to material and thereby maximizing profits.

- Establishing a suitable standard for quality and quantity of food items purchased.

JOB DESCRIPTION OF PURCHASE MANAGER

- Name of the post- Purchase Manager
- Reporting to- General Manager
- Supervising- Purchase officer, Storekeeper, Receiving Clerk

DUTIES AND RESPONSIBILITIES

- Reporting to the senior management
- Maintaining standard operating policy of the hotel
- Management of all the purchase department- receiving, storage, and cellar area
- Purchase of all required commodities
- Conduct market surveys
- Purchase specification, requisition, and purchase order
- Inviting quotations
- Sample testing
- Ensure continuity in effective supply of items to user department
- Research into products, markets, price trends etc
- Co-ordination and liaison with food and beverage department
- Petty cash payments for spot purchase
- Liaison with the accounts, production, controls and marketing department
- Coordinating and conducting briefings, regular meetings with suppliers
- Inviting tenders for contracts
- Renewing the contracts of suppliers
- Ensuring LIFO, FIFO concepts and adhering to the standard policies of the organization
- Providing regular profit or loss and revenue reports to senior management

TYPES OF FOOD PURCHASE

FOOD

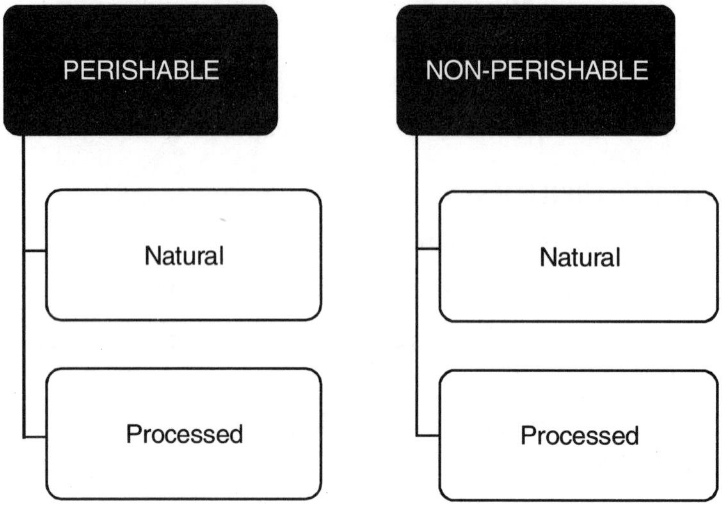

- ***Perishables***

  These are those food items that have limited shelf-life. For example milk, Cream, butter, curd etc.

- ***Non-perishables***

  These are those food items that have extended shelf-life.

  These foods do not decay or spoil without refrigeration.

  For example — canned goods, flour, dry cereals etc.

- ***Natural foods***

  These foods are available in their natural forms as they appear from farms, Orchid etc. Examples are fresh fruits, vegetables, fish, meat etc

- ***Processed foods***

  These are those food items which have undergone some type of treatment on a small and large scale before they are used as basic ingredients.

  For example—pressed rice, cornflakes etc

  - Food stuffs can be placed in 5 basic groups

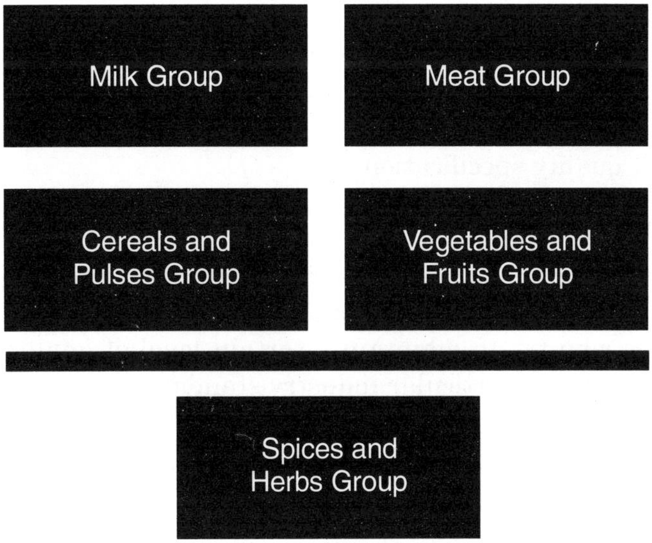

QUALITY PURCHASING

When the purchasing departments are looking at the procurement of materials from suppliers (they have been given some guidance by the manufacturing department, research and development) or the quality department they should include a variety of information about the item to be sourced, such as physical description, dimensional measurements, chemical composition, and performance specifications, standard to conform to, or even the brand name of the product.

PHYSICAL DESCRIPTION

The purchasing department must know the physical attributes of the part they are required to source. For example, if the required material must be made of a certain shade of a blue, then the purchasing department must be able to communicate that requirement to the potential suppliers to ensure that the specification can be met.

CHEMICAL COMPOSITION

This is very important for sourced materials that are used in the chemical process. The quality department should give the purchasing team a detailed list of chemical specifications of the required material. For example, a sourced chemical may be required to have a pH of between 5.6 and 5.9; otherwise the material would not be suitable for the manufacturing processes.

PERFORMANCE SPECIFICATIONS

This quality measurement is key for a business if they are to produce finished goods that are reliable in the eyes of their customers. Therefore it is important for the purchasing department to find suppliers who can provide parts that meet quality specifications.

INDUSTRIAL STANDARDS

Some parts required in the production of finished goods must conform to certain industry standards. These standards are set by a number of trade or industry groups who try to maintain a certain level of quality. By having an item that conforms to a particular industry standard, the customer will have a level of confidence in the product.

FOOD QUALITY

Food quality is the quality characteristics of food that is acceptable to consumers. This includes external factors as appearance (size, shape, color, gloss, and consistency), texture, and flavor; factors such as federal grade standards (e.g. of eggs) and internal (chemical, physical, microbial).

- It is an important aspect of purchasing and quality control can be assured using the following steps—
  - § Food quality also deals with product traceability, (e.g., of ingredient, and packaging suppliers), should a recall of the product be required. It also deals with labeling issues to ensure there is correct ingredient and nutritional information
  - § Setting an accurate specification for each purchase
  - § Checking raw food for quality
  - § Tasting the finished product

QUALITY FACTORS FOR DIFFERENT COMMODITIES

QUANTITATIVE FACTORS

- Number
- Weight
- Volume
- Shape

SENSORY FACTORS

- Appearance

- Odour
- Taste
- Mouth feel

NUTRITIONAL VALUE

- Carbohydrates
- Proteins
- Fats
- Minerals
- Water
- Fibers
- The products must meet the following selection criteria, required by the Institute: sensory analysis, bacteriological and chemical analysis, the nutrition and health claims, and the utilization notice.
- In short, the judgments are based on the following areas: taste, health, convenience, labeling, packaging, environmental friendliness and innovation.
- As many consumers rely on manufacturing and processing standards

DEFINITION OF YIELD

In finance, the term **yield** describes the amount in cash (in percent terms) that returns to the owners of a security. Normally, it does not include the price variations, at the difference of the total return. Yield applies to various stated rates of return on stocks (common and preferred, and convertible), fixed income instruments (bonds, notes, bills, strips, zero coupon), and some other investment type insurance products (e.g. annuities).

• THE VARIOUS TEST TO ARRIVE AT STANDARD YIELDS ARE

- ***Raw food test***: to determine the best cost and weight for fruits and vegetables for specific use
- ***Caused food test***: to determine the yield on actual cost after considering weight, quality, uniformity
- ***Butchering test***: to determine actual portion, costs of meat, poultry, fish and sea food after waste, trim, and by products have been considered
- ***Cooking test***: to determine the final portion cost after cooking, slicing and service less have been considered

- **STANDARD PURCHASE SPECIFICATIONS**
- ***DEFINITION***

Written guidelines that precisely define the operational, physical, and/or chemical characteristics, as well as the quality and quantity of a particular item to be acquired.

Standard purchase specification are concise description of quality, size, weight, or count factor desired for a particular item, Specification buying will give uniformity and consistency to purchasing and receiving, that will aid to maintain a desire food cost and create a standard product.

- ***Objective:***

a) To establish a suitable buying standard for particular commodity for the hotel.

b) To furnish the supplier in writing in specific term the requirement of the hotel.

c) To help in setting the price of a commodity.

d) To obtain a standard product material for F & B Dept.

e) to obtain a standard product so that measurement of performance of departments can be accurate.

For proper and effective control, purchase specification should be used in all purchasing. It helps in bringing uniformity and consistency in buying, which maintains required cost of product. Each specification is determined by purchase manger, Executive chef, and F & B manager as per the catering policies, menu requirement and price range. The specification format is maintained with F & B service and production, receiving, stores department.

The purchase specifications contain:

a) Definition of each item.

b) Grade or brand name of each item

c) Weight, size, or count.

d) Unit against which price should be coated.

e) Special note for commodity.

- **WHO IS IN CHARGE & RESPONSIBLE?**

THE CONTROL PROCESS AND PURCHASING

Goal: ensure a continuing supply of sufficient (quantity)

Of the necessary foods with the required quality and at the best price.

Depending on size and culture of operation, can be:

Owner, chef, purchasing dept., steward.

Critically Important Steps

- determination of quality standards
- Development of standard purchase specs.

• ADVANTAGES OF STANDARD PURCHASE SPECIFICATIONS

1. Forces managers to determine exact requirements in advance for any product
2. Useful in menu preparation
3. Eliminates misunderstandings between stewards and purveyors
4. Circulation of specifications for one product to several purveyors makes competitive bidding possible
5. Eliminates the need for detailed, verbal descriptions of a product each time it is ordered
6. Facilitates checking food as it is received

CENTRALIZED PURCHASING

Advantages

1. Foods and beverages can be purchased at lower prices because of volume
2. Desired quality can be obtained more readily because the purchasing agent has a greater choice of markets
3. Foods can be obtained that meet the purchaser's exact specifications
4. Larger inventories can be maintained, ensuring reliable supply to individual units
5. The possibilities for dishonest purchasing in individual units are greatly reduced

Purchasing is the formal process of buying goods and services. The **purchasing process** can vary from one organization to another, but there are some common key elements.

Purchase orders (PO) can be of various types, including:

- Standard — a onetime buy.
- Planned — an agreement on a specific item at an approximate date.
- Blanket — an agreement on specific terms and conditions: date and quantity and amount are not specified.

Standard Purchasing Procedure

2. Details of purchasing procedure

(1) Purchase request

The specifications and number/quantity and delivery of equipment, devices and materials are determined by the department(s) that will be using the product(s) or materials. The Purchasing Department conducts purchase activities based on purchase requests submitted by the/these department(s).

(2) Selection of companies for estimate submission

The Purchasing Department, at its sole discretion, selects companies from which estimates will be sought. Suppliers are selected from the files of "Companies with Previously Established Business Relationships", "Companies from Which Estimates Can Be Requested" and "Products and Suppliers". Selection is made by comprehensively evaluating such factors as the quality and performance of the equipment, device(s) or materials to be purchased, compatibility with existing facilities, degree of reliability, product requirements including safety, delivery time, the scale of the order, after-sale service and the company's previous business record. As a rule, Osaka Gas asks several companies to submit estimates. However, only one company may be specified for estimate submission in such special cases as those concerned with industrial property rights, those requiring maximum levels of safety that only one specific supplier can ensure, cases where only one specific supplier can assure compatibility with existing facilities, or in case of urgency.

(3) Estimate request

As a rule, when requesting an estimate from a company that it has selected, Osaka Gas will set out a specification from listing Osaka Gas's requirements in respects of quality, performance standard, size, inspection and method of inspection. The selected companies will be asked to submit cost estimates and specifications to Osaka Gas prior to a specified date.

(4) Submission Estimate

Specification sheets submitted by potential suppliers at their own expense are checked by the Purchasing Department and the department(s) that will be using the product(s), in order to determine whether the required standards are met by the product(s). All products must pass this examination. During this process, Osaka Gas may request additions or changes to the specifications.

(5) Negotiation

After valid cost estimates and specifications have been comprehensively evaluated in respect of price, technical requirements, etc. Osaka Gas will commence negotiation with the company with the most attractive proposal to discuss the amount of the contract and other terms and conditions. The selection of such a company shall be made by Osaka Gas at its sole discretion. Contract terms and conditions will be decided upon mutual agreement.

(6) Contract conclusion

The business will be established upon conclusion of a contract, in the form of a written document if necessary. The obligations and liabilities of Osaka Gas arise only when such contract is concluded.

(7) Delivery and inspection

Delivery dates specified in the contract must be strictly observed. Precise details of the delivery schedule will be agreed between the supplier and the relevant department(s) of Osaka Gas. Delivered equipment, device(s) or materials must pass inspections conducted by the relevant department(s) of Osaka Gas. When deemed significant, an interim inspection may be conducted during the manufacturing process.

(8) Payment

Payment will be made according to the payment terms specified in the contract

Purchase orders are normally accompanied by terms and conditions which form the contractual agreement of the transaction. The supplier then delivers the products or service and the customer records the delivery (in some cases this goes through a goods inspection process). An invoice is sent by the supplier which is cross-checked with the purchase order and documents specifying which goods have been received. The payment is then made and transferred to the supplier.

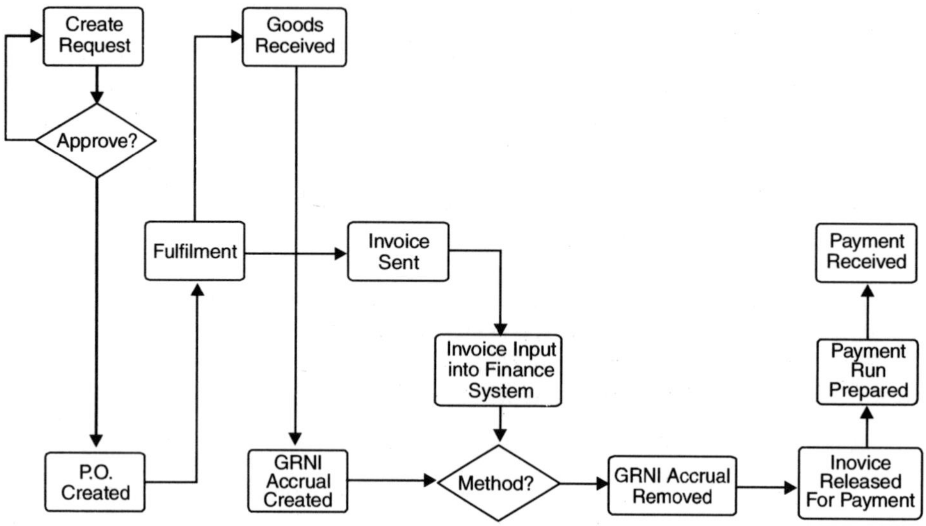

• METHODS OF PURCHASING

Bidding

- Bidding is a purchasing method that involves asking potential vendors to provide cost forecasts and then choosing among available options. Most companies that accept bids decide among available options on the basis of price, but price is not the only criteria. A vendor bid may also include time considerations such as how quickly a vendor can fill an order and how much advance notice he needs. In addition, not every vendor provides products of comparable quality, and sometimes better quality items are worth the additional expense.

Bulk Purchasing

- Purchasing in bulk enables a company to secure low prices by placing substantial orders. Although bulk purchasing offers price advantages, it is not always the best purchasing method to use because you do not need large quantities of every product you purchase. In the case of perishable foods, in particular, it makes sense to limit purchases to the amount you will be able to use before the product spoils. In addition, keeping excessive inventory on hand can raise labor costs because of the need to store and replenish stock.

Petty Cash

- Petty cash is a purchasing method appropriate for small, band-aid purchases, such as paper clips, that one might have been forgotten to include in its office supply order. Petty cash purchases tend to be too small to write a cheque, and are often intermittent in nature. Most businesses keep a petty cash fund with a designated amount of cash, as well as a log for recording the date, item and amount of the petty cash purchase.

Barter

- Barter is a type of purchasing method that involves exchanging products or services other than cash for supplies and materials. The process of bartering can expand your purchasing power because it generally costs less to produce an item than the retail value on which you base your bartering arrangement. For example, if you own a restaurant and you negotiate a barter arrangement with your forager to trade meals for mushrooms, you could trade a dinner that costs you $5.00 to produce for a box of mushrooms that he would typically sell for $15.00.

• THE SOURCES OF SUPPLY

- Whole sellers
- Direct from factory
- Import or international market
- Local market
- Hotel owned factories

Whole sellers

There are opportunities to buy almost anything at wholesale prices, whether you want to buy everyday items or specific products for resale. Once you begin your search, you will see that opportunities to find wholesale buys exist almost everywhere. The process to get started is easy and your contact list of wholesalers will grow quickly.

Direct From Factory

When a hotel purchases goods directly from the manufacture, it is referred to as buying factory direct, or making a direct buys. The factory direct option was facilitated in the 1990s by the development of e-commerce and through distribution of catalogs. Major factories, like Dell Computer, started marketing products directly to their market, rather than going through a traditional tiered sale system. Some consumers prefer to buy goods factory direct, as they tend to be less expensive.

Traditionally, a manufacturer makes items and sells them to a distributor. The distributor, in turn, sells the product to retailers. Each step in the chain increases the end cost of the item, and it also serves as insurance for the step before. For example, a factory can confidently invest a great deal of money in developing and manufacturing a product, because it knows that distributors will purchase it, allowing the factory to recoup its costs immediately. Likewise, a distributor sells to a retailer, covering their expenses, leaving the retailer to sell the product to consumers.

Import or international market

Importing or buying from international market has become necessity In a hotel industry as hotel are dealing day to day with citizens of world and each and every customer is important for the business of hotel. So it becomes mandatory to provide international guests or a guest what ever he or she likes to have. So here arises comes the need of importing goods or products which are not available in own country.

Local market

When it comes to local market, many times in emergency cases hotel buys from the local market at local costs, several reasons behind it could be

- Late delivery of goods from the whole seller
- Unavailability of goods change word regular supplier
- Urgent need of goods
- Less quantity needed

Sometimes hotel need to buy goods from local market when custom or theme goods are required by the hotel

Hotel owned factories

There are many international chain of hotels like oberoi group, Best Western International, Inc, Taj group which own factories which produce high class goods for hotel use only. The goods are made while keeping in mind the theme of the hotel, needs of hotel and standards of the hotel. These goods are not sold in the general market, as they are strictly made for hotel use only, which also saves cost of buying goods and increase the percentage of profit.

PURCHASING BY CONTRACT

Let's first clear what is a "contract"?

A written or spoken agreement, especially one concerning employment, sales, or tenancy that is intended to be enforceable by law.

Then what is **"Purchasing by Contract"**?

All the purchasing done by the party or organization from other party or supplier at regular interval under laws, agreement and duties of a contract is known as purchasing by contract

TYPES OF CONTRACTS—

A. Fixed-Price Contracts

A fixed-price contract—places responsibility on the contractor for the delivery of the product or the complete performance of the services or construction in accordance with the contract terms at a price which is firm or may be subject to contractually specified adjustments. The fixed-price contract is appropriate for use when the extent and type of work necessary to meet University requirements can be reasonably specified and the cost can be reasonably estimated, as is generally the case for construction or standard commercial products. A fixed-price type of contract is the only type of contract that can be used in competitive sealed bidding.

B. Requirements Contract

This type of contract provides for filling all actual purchase requirements of specific supplies or services of designated organization or hotel activities during a specified contract period with deliveries to be scheduled by the timely placement of orders with the contractor. For such a contract, an estimated total quantity is stated in the Invitation for Bids for the information of prospective contractors and should reflect the organization's estimated use of such supplies or services as realistically as possible. The estimate may be obtained from the records of previous requirements

Clauses of a purchase contract—

- The period
- Estimated quantities
- Reservation of the establishment to decide a contract between suppliers
- Removal of rejected food by supplier
- Containers chargeable
- Power to purchase in default
- In case of dispute – an agreed party
- Indemnity against damage
- Prevention of corruption

Purchase Order

#0000

P.O. number must appear on all invoices and packages

Send Invoices To:	Your Company Name Attn: Accounts Payable Your Street Your Town

Date : ____________

Vendor : ____________________________

____

____

Quantity	Unit	Category#	Description	Unit Price	Total

Total: ____________

____________________________ ____________

Authorized Signature Date

- The place of delivery
- Invoices
- Payment of invoice
- Service of notice to break a contract

PERIODICAL PURCHASING

The requirements of the establishment are periodically estimated and regular orders are placed on a daily / weekly / monthly basis to ensure that's stocks should be available up to par stock and for emergency usage. A quotation is prepared according to the need or requirement, the budget, and the space available for storage this type of buying is mostly used for grocery type commodities

• DAILY MARKET QUOTATION / BY REQUIREMENT

This method is used to purchase goods on a daily basis sometimes some goods are received in lesser amount as per daily requirements so it become mandatory to order again some quantity of that particular good on emergency basis / on receipt of "daily market list" the purchase office contacts on telephone, each approved suppliers and asks to quote price for each of the item required. The quoted prices are entered on the daily market list and a decision is taken by the purchase office as to where to place the order of each item.

DAILY MARKET LIST

S.NO	ITEMS	QUANTITY	QUALITY WANTED	SUPPLIER		
				A	B	C
1	DAIRY Eggs Yoghurt Milk					
2	MEAT, POULTRY Chicken Ham sausages					
3	SEA FOOD Fish Prawns Oysters					
4	VEGETABLES Onions Potatoes Parsley Bell peppers					
5	BREADS Bread loafs Bread rolls Whole wheat bread Fruit bread					

OPEN MARKET PURCHASING

Purchase of goods, usually in smaller quantities or in an emergency, without contract or negotiations

- Quotations are asked from the various suppliers of commodities
- The prices are compared and order is placed to the firm keeping in mind the price and quantity provisions
- **Cash and carry method** – This is one of the famous and suitable methods for small and medium sized establishment there is complete freedom for purchasing from the market at competitive price. In this caterer has to pay cash for all items purchased and provide own transport
- **"Paid reserve" method** – this method is used when it is ensure the quantity of supply of an item for the menu which is of particular importance for a special restaurant /establishment, such as, jumbo size prawns, frozen fillets of beef etc.
- **"Cost plus" method** – this a more suitable for nonprofit catering institutions such hospitals, boarding houses etc the approved suppliers is paid exactly the same price that he paid for the commodities plus an agreed percentage to include the cost of handling, delivery charges and a margin of profit.
- **"Total supply" method** – there are some suppliers who are able to offer to a full supply service of all commodities. A food and beverage establishment may agree for a supplier. this system has the advantage of only having to negotiate with one supplier, a reduced volume of paper work.

STANDING ORDER PURCHASES

Purchase order covering repeated deliveries of goods or services in specified quantities, at specified prices, and according to a specified schedule. As in many 5 star hotel give the supplier a approximate schedule of delivery of requirement if any changes further informed by the purchase department to the supplier.

CENTRALIZED PURCHASING

This system is popular in chain operations a purchasing system in which all the departments of a company with a wide geographical distribution can make purchases through a common purchasing organization. Centralized purchasing aids finding the best deals with local vendors for the corresponding location of the company department. Avoids duplicity of orders and promotes benefits arising from the high volume bulk discounts, lower transportation and inventory costs, organized transactions and improved vendor relationships. Usually located at company headquarters. Opposite of decentralized purchasing.

ADVANTAGES OF CENTRALIZED PURCHASING

The various advantages of centralized purchasing are as follows:

1. Fixation of responsibility: The purchase department can be held responsible for inefficient purchasing.
2. Economy: Economy in compilation of records is achieved as all records of purchase are kept at one place.
3. Specialized knowledge: Concentration of expert purchasing staff in one department develops specialized knowledge and skill.
4. Favorable terms: There may be favorable terms with reduced cost due to more trade discount, quantity discount and less transport cost because materials are purchased in bulk quantities.
5. Better Control: Better control on purchasing is possible under centralized purchasing. There is no chance of reckless purchase since one person is authorized to make purchase for the whole organization.
6. Firm Policy: A firm policy can be initiated under centralized purchasing, this makes possible in reduction of prices of various commodities.

DISADVANTAGES OF CENTRALIZED PURCHASING

The main disadvantages of centralized purchasing are as under:

1. Delay: Centralized planning causes delay as plants may be situated in different places. It is really very difficult to consolidate the requirements of all items different factories and then place orders with suppliers.
2. High initial cost: It leads to high initial cost because a specialized purchase department for purchase of material has to be established.
3. Local Purchase: The benefits arising out of local purchase cannot be availed of where there is centralized purchase in operation.
4. Emergency Purchase: In case of centralized purchasing, emergency purchase cannot be made.
5. Communication difficulty: This system of purchase leads to communication difficulty between centralized purchase office and the plants.
6. Less flexible: The purchasing procedure under centralized purchasing is less flexible.

Once a supplier is chosen the following points must also be considered before orders are placed:

- Classification of products
- Purchase order must be confirmed in writing
- Responsibility of purchasing
- Stock life of products
- Money available to market purchasers- cash flow

The quantity regarded will depend on:

- Existing stock levels
- Expected volume of business
- Current market prices and trends
- Tariffs
- Storage space available

METHODS OF PURCHASING IN HOTELS

- Contract Purchasing
- Periodical Purchasing
- Open Market Purchasing
- Standard Order Purchasing
- Centralized Purchasing

ORDERING COST

Ordering costs are costs of ordering a new batch of raw materials. These include cost of placing a purchase order, costs of inspection of received batches, documentation costs, etc.

Ordering costs vary inversely with carrying costs. It means that the more orders a business places with its suppliers, the higher will be the ordering costs. However, more orders mean smaller average inventory levels and hence lower carrying costs.

It is important for a business to minimize the sum of these costs which it does by applying the economic order quantity model.

- ***Example***

Azer Gas is a company engaged in gas distribution to households and businesses through its network of pipelines in Azerbaijan. The company expands its pipelines every now and then. Installation of pipelines involves use of specialized high quality pipes, customized valves and other spares and loose tools. Azer Gas has only a few suppliers who produce these customized tools. Azerbaijani government regulations require the company to advertise in three national and two international newspapers before placing a purchase order. This will cost $200, 000 per order. The suppliers have to modify their own production plans and they charge an amount of $2 million regardless of the size of order. The opportunity cost of staff time spent on drafting the tender documents is estimated at $250, 000. Related legal costs are $50, 000. In each procurement Azer Gas hires a firm for inspection at a flat fee of $100, 000. Bank charges an amount of $3, 000 as documentation charges.

In this situation, Azer Gas ordering costs are $2, 603, 000 per order (advertisement costs of $200, 000 + customization cost of $2, 000, 000 + opportunity cost of staff time of $250, 000 + legal costs of $50, 000 + inspection costs of $100, 000 + bank charges of $3, 000).

Since there are constant improvements in the related technology, the most significant related carrying cost is obsolescence. Other carrying costs which Azer Gas would have to trade-off against the ordering costs include the opportunity cost of capital tied up in the expensive tools, the cost of wear and tear of the tools, etc.

CARRYING COSTS

Carrying costs are costs which a business incurs on maintaining its intended level of inventories. These include storage costs (such as warehouse rent, fire insurance, spoilage costs, etc) and opportunity cost of capital tied up in inventories.

It is important for a business to keep track of its carrying costs because they are significant component of total cost of inventories.

Since, there is an inverse relationship between carrying costs and ordering costs, businesses normally apply the economic order quantity model to minimize their total cost of inventories by reaching a trade-off between both of these costs.

• ***Example***

Jadeja Textiles is a business engaged in textile manufacturing in Indian state of Punjab. Their key raw materials include cotton and artificial fibres. They pay an amount of INR 1,200,000 as annual rent for its raw materials warehouse. Cotton occupies 80% of the floor space of the warehouse. They maintains an average inventory of cotton of INR 20,000,000 and average inventory of artificial fibres of INR 10,000,000 and their cost of capital is 12%. They pay INR 200,000 as annual fire insurance. Calculate the annual carrying cost of cotton.

In the example, the carrying costs of cotton include the proportionate rent of warehouse, proportionate fire insurance and the opportunity cost of capital. Proportionate rent of warehouse is INR 960,000 (80% of INR 1,200,000), proportionate fire insurance is INR 133,333 (200,000/(20M+10M)*20M) and opportunity cost of capital is INR 2,400,000 (12% of INR 20M). Total carrying costs of cotton is hence INR 3,493,333.

PURCHASE ORDER FORMS

This is another important document to be issued for all items ordered. This should be prepared listing all items ordered, delivery time, terms of payment, the agreed price and other conditions/instructions.

ECONOMIC ORDER QUANTITY (EOQ)

The Economic Order Quantity (EOQ) is the number of units that a company should add to inventory with each order to minimize the total costs of holding inventory—such as holding cost, order cost, and shortage cost. The EOQ is used as part of a continuous review inventory system in which the level of inventory is monitored at all times and a fixed quantity is ordered each time the inventory level reaches a specific reorder point. The EOQ provides a model for calculating the appropriate reorder point and the optimal reorder quantity to ensure the instantaneous replenishment of inventory with no shortages. It can be a valuable tool for small business owners who need to make decisions about how much inventory to keep on hand, how many items to order each time, and how often to reorder to incur the lowest possible costs.

The EOQ model assumes that demand is constant, and that inventory is depleted at a fixed rate until it reaches zero. At that point, a specific number of items arrive to return the inventory to its beginning level. Since the model assumes instantaneous replenishment, there are no inventory shortages or associated costs. Therefore, the cost of inventory under the EOQ model involves a tradeoffs between inventory holding costs (the cost of storage, as well as the cost of tying up capital in inventory rather than investing it or using it for other purposes) and order costs (any fees associated with placing orders, such as delivery charges). Ordering a large amount at one time will increase a small business's holding costs, while making more frequent orders of fewer items will reduce holding costs but increase order costs. The EOQ model finds the quantity that minimizes the sum of these costs.

Purchase Order

Date: **P.O. #:** **Customer ID:**

Vendor	**Ship To**
Company Name	Customer/Company Name
Address	Address
Phone #	Phone #
Email	Email

Shipping Method	Delivery Terms	Delivery Date

Product Code	Description	Quantity	Price	Total
			Total	

Special Instructions	Date	Approval Signature
	Purchaser Signature	Title

Purchase Order Request Form

Req. No. ____________ Purchase Order No. ____________

Account No. ____________ Account Name ____________

Professor's Name ____________ Signature ____________

Your Name ____________ Your Email ____________ Your Phone Number ____________

Date ____________

Special Instructions:

Item No.	Description	Quantity	Unit (each, pkg, case)	Per-Unit Price	Line Item Total Price

☐ In Stock ☐ Lead Time ____________ **Total Price** ____________

Shipping Preference ☐ Ground ☐ Express

Complete Name of Vendor: ____________ Name of Contact: ____________

Address of Vendor: ____________ Contact's phone number: ____________

____________ Contact's fax number: ____________

Please attach any web printout or email or faxed quotation received from vendor.

The basic EOQ relationship is shown below. Let us look at it assuming we have a painter using 3, 500 gallons of paint per year, paying $5 a gallon, a $15 fixed charge every time he/she orders, and an inventory cost per gallon held averaging $3 per gallon per year.

The relationship is $TC = PD + HQ/2 + SD/Q$ where

- TC is the total annual inventory cost—to be calculated.
- P is the price per unit paid—assumes $5 per unit.
- D is the total number of units purchased in a year—assumes 3, 500 units.
- H is the holding cost per unit per year—assumes $3 per unit per annum.
- Q is the quantity ordered each time an order is placed—initially assume 350 gallons per order.
- S is the fixed cost of each order—assumes $15 per order.

PRACTICAL PROBLEMS

- Transportation strike affects the delivery of the items at the delivery point;
- The availability of the stock from different sources costs high carriage charges;
- Labour strikes affects the production and ultimately the delivery drastically;
- The desired quality not delivered as promised earlier by the supplier;
- Different areas have different prices of the product, carriage charges and labour charges which leads to the ultimate increase in the cost of purchasing;
- Cost of import also leads to increase the final cost of the product.

QUESTIONNAIRE

1. What do you understand by purchasing control?
2. Discuss the aims of purchasing policy?
3. Give the job description and responsibilities of a purchase manager in a five star hotel?
4. What are different types of food purchase?
5. What do you understand by quality purchasing? Discuss.
6. Discuss the different food quality factors for different commodities?
7. Define yield. What are the different tests to arrive at standard yield?
8. Define standard purchase specification. What are its advantages and disadvantages?
9. What is purchasing procedure and what are different methods of food purchasing?
10. Discuss the various sources of supply in detail.
11. What are the different methods of purchasing used in hotels?
12. Differentiate between centralized purchasing and contract purchasing.
13. Differentiate between carrying cost and ordering cost.
14. Write short notes on:
    - Economic order quantity (EOQ)
    - Open market purchasing
    - Standard yield
    - Standard purchase specifications (SPS)

UNIT 3

RECEIVING CONTROL

AIMS OF RECEIVING

The quantity of goods delivered matches the quantity which has been ordered. It means that all goods will have to be weighed or control.

1. The prices stated on the delivery note are in accordance is not in accordance with the prices on purchase order form.
2. When the quantity and quality of food ordered is not in accordance with the purchase order or an item is omitted from the order a request for credit note is raised by the receiving clerk.
3. An accurate record is maintained in the goods receiving book recording details of the delivery.

Receiving merchandise is an accounting function and must be completely separated from purchasing to make collusion between the two functions difficult. The duty performed by the receiving personnel includes:

1. Scale being properly adjusted
2. Each item weighed net without wrapping, ice container or packing material. Special items like fresh fruits that bruise easily are handled with care so as not to damage the food. A record of the weight of various empty containers is kept for easier checking or net weight of fruit in the container. This will avoid employing the containers which might spoil the food.
3. Items are counted individually when received.
4. Goods purchased in cases are tested to ascertain that the entire content is of the specified quality.
5. Items purchased against standard purchase specification.

6. Items purchased for quality and uniformity- i.e. if necessary by consulting the chef or purchasing agent.
7. Perishables must be dated and priced on the container with wax crayon or tagged.
8. Request for credit immediately issued where the weight or count is less than invoiced or where inferiority quality necessities a return of merchandise.
9. Consistently late shipments brought to the attention of the purchasing department.
10. The purchasing deparment appraised of any dealer whose merchandise is repeatedly substandard in quality or sort in quantity.
11. All goods are received at the centralized receiving department.
12. Goods must be checked against invoice and clearly examined as to price, quantity, quality or weight.
13. The receiver must sign and stamp his name in invoice in order to acknowledge proper receipt of goods.
14. Groceries and other invoices are posted daily by the purchasing agent office to the receiving sheet.
15. The sale value of tags must agree with the invoice. The upper part of tag is kept in the store room and this is sent together with the invoice is sent the following morning to the Food and Beveage Controller Office.
16. Tags for meat and all form of fish items are issued daily by the food store room clerk. Tags give the following information:
    a) Date of receipt
    b) Type of meat or fish
    c) Unit Price
    d) Average price per price of products.

RECEIVING CLERK JOB DESCRIPTION

DUTIES AND RESPONSIBILITIES

1. Accurate physical receiving of materials/products in order to maintain integrity of Inventory Control
2. Insures delivery of materials/products to the proper department
3. Schedules all inbound deliveries; ensures purchase order number is on all paperwork

4. Receives product deliveries
5. Maintains a record and checks the quantity and quality of goods received
6. Inspects, accept or rejects inbound shipments
7. Communicates and co-ordinates with appropriate buyer for product returns/repair
8. Properly inputs received material into the system and forwards proper documentation
9. Delivers product to appropriate personnel
10. Performs other duties as assigned to meet business needs
11. Establishes and maintains effective working relationships with other employees, supervisors and managers
12. Maintains safe work environment according to all department procedures
13. Receives product deliveries, ensuring order and invoice accuracy.
14. Move items into appropriate locations for stocking or back-stock
15. Ensures exterior doors are locked and secure when not in use.
16. Ensures only authorized personnel enter receiving area.
17. Stocks, rotates, and merchandises products as needed according to department.
18. Trains other staff as required.
19. Knows and adheres to quality standards for customer service as outlined
20. Maintains back stock areas according to department standards.
21. Receives products, insures invoice accuracy, and assists with ordering, receiving and stocking of goods.

EQUIPMENT REQUIRED FOR RECEIVING

All goods purchased via a Purchase Order by the procurement department are centrally received at a particular receiving station. All deliveries and returns are processed through the Property Control Department. If vendors make purchase order deliveries directly to the departments, the department should redirect the delivery to the concerned department

A receiving report is made for each item received by the Receiving Department. The receiving report is used to ensure items are paid for in a timely manner. It is necessary to have a receiving report properly prepared, verified, and submitted to Accounts Payable within 24 hours of receipt of goods. The receiving personnel are responsible for the completion of the receiving report. Additionally, it is within the receiving section that items to be tagged as Fixed Assets are identified, recorded, and tagged.

OVERAGES, SHORTAGES, AND DAMAGES

All items delivered to the Receiving department are to be opened and inspected within 24 hours of delivery. Items received are to be compares with the Hotel's purchase order to confirm that they are in a good condition, when sent to the concerned department.

On receipt of items, the requestor is urged to immediately check the contents of shipments for conformity with the packing slips. If there is shortage, overage, damage or incorrect item, the receiving section should be notified with the immediate effect.

RETURNS TO VENDORS

No shipments will be returned without approval of procurement. Procurement is responsible for all adjustments with suppliers and claims against carriers. Departments are asked not to return the items purchased through procurement directly to vendors, but rather through the procurement department. Adherence to this procedure will permit the procurement department to properly document to the appropriate accounts. The following procedure is used to return the item to a vendor:

1. Complete the "Return to Vendor" form and forward it to the Procurement Department
2. The procurement department will conduct the necessary co-ordination among the vendor and carrier.
3. The department returning the items will be responsible for shipping costs if the items are returned due to a fault.
4. The vendor is responsible for the shipping costs if the items are returned due to no fault of the hotel
5. The procurement department will co-ordinate with the Accounts payable so that payment access can be addressed.
6. The procurement department will co-ordinate with property control to pick up the items to be returned.

   NOTE: Damaged and/or non-confirming items are to be noted in the comment section of the Receiving report.

Items that are initially inspected in the receiving section and are found to be damaged or they do not confirm to the Purchase order specifications, will not be accepted. The requesting department will be notified. The goods are held in the receiving section of the disposition of the damaged/non-conforming goods (i.e. mail back to vendor, hold for vendor pick-up, etc.). The procurement department will confirm all vendor contacts in writing.

Equipments required are:

1. **Weighing Scale**- Small/big: To check the quantities of the received goods.
2. **Platforms**: Where the goods can be inspected for quality.
3. **Writing Tables**: For doing paper work.
4. **Racks**: For storing empty returnable boxes and card board boxes and other material.
5. **Storage Container**: For storage of products in unsealed packge containers.
6. Waste bins with lids.
7. Trolleys for the movement of food from receiving area to storage facilities.
8. Stacking trolleys.
9. **First aid box**: For the unexpected things that can happen due to delivery vehicles and movement, lifting of heavy items, breakages of containers etc.
10. Computers and Stationary items.
11. Invoice/Delivery Note
12. Every time food is delivered to an establishment it is accompanied by a document that lists the items being delivered. The document is normally an invoice which is same as a bill.
13. It is prepared in duplicate/triplicate. The original and second copy is sent along with the supply and is given to the receiving clerk who would sign or stamp the invoice.

INVOICE

Date-2/12/13

Quick Check Co Ltd. S.No.

New Delhi

To- Hotel Le Meridian

S.No.	Description	Unit	Quantity	Unit Price	Total	Remark
1.	Chicken Whole	Kg.	80	60	480	—

Received By........... Signature..........

DELIVERY NOTES

A **delivery note** explains what the contents of a package are.

If some goods that were ordered are not enclosed (due to lack of stock, unavailability, etc.) they will also be listed on the delivery note. This way the recipient will have an overview of what they ordered and what has actually been sent to them.

The receiver checks the **delivery note** (supply note/order which comes along with the goods) and the copy of the purchase order along with purchase specification to ensure that the goods are received late then they are not accepted. For example 1000 kilogram of chicken is required for a party to commence at 6 p.m. and the supply of chicken comes at 4 p.m. If there is any difference in-between the delivery note and the purchase order and purchase specification then this must be immediately brought to the notice of supplier and purchaser and recorded on the supply order and if the supplied goods are unacceptable then they must be returned immediately with remarks that the goods are not as per the order. This is also to be note that kitchens can not prepare food in two hours. A local purchasing of chicken must have to be made. Any variation in supply of goods, the purchase officer should be immediately informed so that appropriate action can be initiated against the suppliers.

The **delivery note** is normal duplicate. The top copy is retained in the receiving depatment and the second is signed by the senior member of the receiving department and returned to the deivery man, in case the quantity of items delivered is less than that stated on delivery note and the items are not acceptable, the reciving department must obtain a credit note.

All deliveries of goods received must be recorded daily on goods inward book. These goods may be categorized as:

- Food items
- Beverage and tobacco including the containers or empties receive and returned.
- Non-food and beverage items.

The originals of all food and beverage delivery notes must be passed on to the and beverage controller. Finally these are sent to the bought ledger where all invoice will be attached with the respective purchase order form and delivery.

ABC HOTELS LTD.

Delivery Note

Hotel

Customer's Copy

To

No. ....

Date..............

Order No.	Quantity	Description	Unit Value	Remarks
Delivered by Signature				Received by Signature

ABC HOTELS LTD.

REQUEST FOR CREDIT MEMO/NOTE

No. ....

Date ....

To

....

....

PLEASE ISSUE CREDIT MEMO FOR ITEMS LISTED BELOW

Qty.	Unit	Item	Cost	
			Unit Rs.	Total Rs.
FOOD & BEVERAGE CONTROLLER	ACCOUNT DEPTT.	VAN DRIVER GOOD RECIVED	REQUESTED BY	

Receiving Officer's Signature		Date:
Supplier's Name	Order No.	Supply Order Remarks No.

Goods Received Book

HENRY HILSON HOTEL **DATE Oct. 3**

BEVERAGE RECEIVING REPORT

							Purchase Journal Distribution			
Distributor	Item	Quantity Received	Purchase Unit	Size	Unit Cost	Total Cost	Wines	Beers	Spirits	Mixers
A&C Suppliers	Old Crow	6	case	750 ml	$ 155.50	$ 932.40			$ 932.40	
A&C Suppliers	Beefeater	2	case	750 ml	$ 179.40	$ 358.80			$ 358.80	
Blue Distributors	Budweiser	12	case	375 ml	$ 11.95	$ 143.40		$ 143.40		
Canada Dry	Tonic	7	case	250 ml	$ 9.00	$ 63.00				$ 63.00
Krumpf Importers	Moselle	4	case	750 ml	$ 60.00	$ 240.00	$ 240.00			
Krumpf Importers	Chateau Rue	2	case	750 ml	$ 105.00	$ 210.00	$ 210.00			
Total						$1,947.60	$ 450.00	$ 143.40	$1,291.20	$ 63.00

BEVERAGE RECEIVING REPORT

THE INVOICE/BILL

Information is a document containing detailed information about the food deliveries. It is presented to the reciving clerk in duplicate by the person making the delivery who excepts the receiving clerk to sign and return the second copy, thus acknowledge to the purveyor or that the hotel has received the commodities listed.The original **inovice** in a bill that must be paid and must be routed through accounts department for paying the bill.

Every time food is delivered to an establishment, it should be accompanied by a document that lists the items being delivered. For food, the document is normally an **invoice**, which is the same as a bill.

An **invoice** is usually presented to the receiving clerk in duplicate by the person making the delivery, who will expect the receiving clerk to sign and return the second copy. This serves as an acknowledgment to the purveyor that the establishment has received the products listed on the **invoice**. The original is, in effect, a bill that must be routed to the bookkeeper or other individual responsible for paying bills.

This routing procedure is dealt with later in this chapter. The acceptance of invoices not listing prices should be discouraged: Prices should be checked as the food products are received. Otherwise, it is possible that a purveyor may bill at the wrong prices, either by accident or by design.

The receiving clerk shouldrubber stamp all the inovice which contain the following information:

- Date
- Steward
- Received
- Price and extensions
- Verified ok for payment

The stamping of an inovice is useful for the following reason

- It provides verification of the date on which food items have been received. It provides signature of the receiving clerk and voucher for the accuracy of quantities, qualities and price.
- It provides for the Seward's signature acknowledging that the food has been delivered.
- It provides for food controller verification of the airthmetical accuracy of the bill.
- It provide for the signature approval of the bill for the payment by an authorised idividual before a check is drawn.

To check deliveries thoroughly following supplies and equipment must be made available to the receiving personnel:

- Copies of all standard purchase specification.
- Equipment such as
  - Platform scale
  - Hanging scale
  - Hanging racks

- Stationary items such as
    - Forms
    - Tags
    - Rubber stamps
    - Office supplies

INVOICE MEMO

Invoice
Market Price Meat Co
300 Market St.
New York, NY

TO The Graduate Restaurant　　Date June 11

Quantity	*Unit*	*Description*	*Unit Price*	*Amount*
30	lbs.	Strip Steak	10.45	$ 313.50
10	lbs.	Breast of Veal	12.35	$ 123.50
				$ 437.00

BEVERAGE INVOICE

To: Henry Hilson Hotel
1066 West 41st Street
New York, NY 10098

INVOICE # 639-A142
TERMS C.O.D.

DATE Oct. 3　ORDER # C267　ACCOUNT # H108　SHIP Truck

Item No.	Quantity Ordered	Quantity Shipped	Purchase Unit	Bottle Size	Description	Unit Price	Total Price
458	6	6	case	750 ml	Old Crow bourbon	$ 155.40	$ 932.40
376	2	2	case	750 ml	Beefeater gin	$ 179.40	$ 358.80
						Total	$ 1,291.20

HOTEL BILL RECEIPT FORMAT

Hotel Bill Receipt Template

Hotel Bill Receipt

Name of the Hotel_________________
Address: _________________
Contact number: _________________

Bill No: [specify an unique number]	
Number of hotel rooms booked	
Room rate	
Room Number	
Check in Time and date:	[specify time in _____: ______pm/am and date in dd-mm-yy]
Check out Time and date:	[specify time in _____: ______pm/am and date in dd-mm-yy]

Room boarded by: __________ [name of the individual]
Address: ____________________[address of the same]
Phone number: ____________

Name of the food services	Quantity per unit	Total amount

Miscellaneous or other hotel services	Rate of each services	Total amount

Percentage of sales tax: ________________ [%]
Grand total amount: ________________ [inclusive of all taxes]
Discount offered: __________[mention if any concession is offered by the hotel authority to the individual]

Payment Mode: [mention the mode of payment by which the individual paid off the charges that are incurred for taking the hotel services]

- Cash / Cheque
- Debit/ Credit Cards

Signature of the hotel in-charge /manager:
Signature of the customer:

----------------THANK YOU FOR YOUR VISIT----------------

More at **invoice-template.org**

CREDIT NOTE

A **credit note** is a monetray instrument issued by a seller that allows buyers to purchase an item or service from that seller on a future date; i.e. A gift card or store card credit. **Credit notes** may be issued by a seller as a goodwill gesture to a buyer who whises to return previously purchased merchandise (instead of cash replayment) in circumstances where the original sales agreement did not include an explicit refund policy for returned items. In such circumstances, a credit note of value equal to the price of the returnred item is usually issued allowing the buyer to exchange his purchase for other items available with the sale.

A **credit Note** or **Credit Memo** can also be used to adjust or rectify error made in sales invoice which has alerady been processed and sent to a customer. If you have alerady sent an invoice to a customer but now need to provide a credit for that invoice, you would send them a **Credit Note** or **Credit Memo**. You can think of a credit note as a "negative invoice"?

A **credit Note** can also be raised for returned goods. After the sale, if the customer is not happy with the goods for verious reasons like damage, expired he would return the goods This transaction has to reversed for accounting purposes and a special type called credit note can be used.

A **credit note** can be issued to correct a mistake if the invoice has been overstated or to reimburse the buyer completely if the goods have been returned. If you return goods to a supplier or if a customer returns goods to you for a full or partial credit, a credit note must be issued so that you or your customer can process this and adjust your accounts accordingly.

If you have paid the **invoice** before the goods arrive and then have to return them due to damage or unsuitability then a credit note can be issued if you intend to buy more from that supplier as this can be offset against future purchases which in some cases would be the suppliers preference or you may require a refund of your payment.

XYZ HOTEL

CREDIT NOTE

Item	**Delivery Note No./ Supply Order No.**	**Amount Rs.**	**Remarks**
Receiving Officer's Signature			Delivery Man's Signature

RECEIVING PROCEDURE

Receiving merchandise is an accounting function and must be kept completely separated from purchasing to make collusion between the two functions difficult. The Food and Beverage Controller must verify that proper receiving routines are in effect which includes-

- Scale being properly adjusted
- Each item weighed net without wrapping, ice container or packaging materials. Special items like fresh fruit that bruise easily are handled with care so as not to damage the food. A record of the weight of the fruit in the container. This will avoid employing the containers which spoil the food.
- Items are counted individually when received
- Goods purchased in cases are tested to ascertain that the entire contents are of the specified quality.
- Items checked against standard purchase specifications.
- Items checked for quality and uniformity- if necessary by consulting the chef or purchasing agent.
- Perishables must be dated and priced on the container with wax crayon or tagged if they lack suitable surfaces for direct marking.
- Amount of merchandise delivered compared to the amount ordered.
- Request for credit immediately issued where the weight or count is less than invoiced or where inferior quality necessitates a return of merchandise.
- Insistence that any changes on invoices or receiving slips are initialled by the delivery man.
- Memo invoice made out when no bill or delivery slip accompanies the merchandise
- Consistently late shipments must be brought to the attention of the purchasing department.

The receiving practice must be clearly stated and all employees related to receiving must adhere to the system adopted for the hotel—

- All goods are received at the centralised receiving department.
- Deliveries must be accompanied by the covering invoice. In case the invoice is not obtained a 'memorandum invoice' has to be written out by the receiver.
- Separate invoices for food, beverages, maintenance items, operating and cleaning suppliers are requested.

- Goods must be checked aginst invoice and clearly examined as to—
  1. Price
  2. Quality
  3. Quantity or Weight

The value of each case must be broken down for each individual container and marked accordingly before being stored.

- The receiver must stamp and sign his name on invoice in order to acknowledge proper receipt of goods.
- Groceries and other invoices are posted daily by the purchasing agent/ officer's office to the report /sheet.
- Tags for meat and all forms of fish items are issued daily by the Food Storeroom clerk.
  1. Date of receipt
  2. Purveyor
  3. Type of meat
  4. Unit price
  5. Average price per piece of product
- The Food and Beverage Controller spot checks receiving procedure. In case of doubt about the quality of food, the executive chef must be consulted.

The procedure of receiving of goods may briefly outline as:

- Checking for quality against the purchase order
- Checking for quality against purchase specification and raising a credit note wherever there are any discrepancies

MEAT TAG

Tagging is done for expensive items such as special processed meats such as ham, fish such as smoked salmon, poultry and shell fish etc.

This serves many purposes such as:

- Control of expensive food
- Receiving department weighs and records each item against the specific weight range
- Assists in obtaining a more accurate daily food cost percentage figure
- Assists in controlling the stock level of these items

Date received **No. 100**
Item
Grade
Weight
Date issued
Date used

In addition meat tag serves the following purpose:

- To control an expensive item of food or meat
- To ensure that receiving clerk weighs each time
- To check individual weight of each item against the specification weight
- To provide a reference number to aid issuing to the kitchen and when yield testing

The tagging system is operated as follows:

- After checking the item or the receipt, a tag is made out for each item. Necessary information is taken from the invoice or delivery note.
- Separate the tag along the perforation. The control office copy being sent to the control with the invoice and delivery note.
- Kitchen copy is attached by string or wire to the food item.
- When the item is issued at a later date, to the kitchen for use the tag attached to the item is removed and sent to control with the date of issue filled therein.
- The control office maintains a Meat Tag Reconciliation Form. It contains the record of tags received from the receiving department and from the kitchen. The total value of each specific experience item could help for:
    1. Facilitating daily purchases
    2. Daily issues to the kitchen for immediate use

3. Balance indicated by the reconciliation form would give the stock value of those items.

DAILY RECEIVING REPORT

All purchases are broken down into the following categories-

DIRECT PURCHASES

1. All dairy product
2. Breads
3. Ice creams
4. Fresh fish
5. Vegetables
6. Fresh perishable fruits.

STORE PURCHASES

1. Canned purchases
2. All tagged goods
3. Butter
4. Egg, etc.
   - Sale tax will be recorded in the 'direct' column
   - Credit and debit adjustments are recorded under the category concerned.

GOODS RECEIVED BOOKS

All goods received are recorded in the **Goods Received Book**. This remains as a permanent record of all the goods received by the receiving department. For each day a separate goods received book's page is allotted. This is usually maintained by small hotels. Larger hotels prefer to maintain analytical receiving book. Separate columns are made for meat, chicken, vegetables, frozen food, milk, grocery, etc. This gives information at a glance that how much quantity under various head is received on a particular day.

EQUIPMENTS REQUIRED BY RECEIVING DEPARTMENT

The equipments required by the receiving department can be broadly divided into major equipments and minor equipments. The receiving department should be well equipped with the various equipment so that the goods can be received efficiently made both the quantity as well as quality can be inspected.

RECEIVING CLERK'S DAILY REPORT

Receiving Clerk's Daily Report						**NO.**	**1**	
						DATE	**June 11**	
						Purchase Journal Distribution		
			Unit		Total	Food	Food	
Quantity	Unit	Description	Price	Amount	Amount	Direct	Stores	Sundries
		Market Price						
		Meats						
30	lbs.	Strip Steak	$ 10.45	$ 313.50				
10	lbs.	Breast of Veal	$ 12.35	$ 123.50				
					$ 437.00		$ 437.00	
		Ottman Meats						
15	lbs.	Pork Tenderloins	$ 6.35	$ 92.25	$ 92.25		$ 92.25	
		Jones Produce						
		& Fruit						
	Crate	Lettuce	$ 16.50	$ 16.50				
	Bag	Onions	$ 12.75	$ 12.75				
	Box	Grapefruit	$ 18.30	$ 18.30				
	Crate	Peaches	$ 22.60	$ 22.60				
					$ 70.15	$ 70.15		
				$ 599.40	$ 599.40	$ 70.15	$ 529.25	

GOODS RECEIVED BOOK IS PURCHASE ORDERS

Purchase officer places the purchase order with the suppliers giving details of the quantity-and quality of items required to be delivered. The purchase orders are made out with five copies, each copy being colour coded to aid the correct distribution of them. The colour coding may differ from organization to organization.

White Copy (original) sent to Supplier

Yellow copy- sent to accounts department

Green copy- sent to receiving department

Pink copy- retained by the purchasing department

Off white copy- retained in the purchasing office and kept in date order wise and retained till the goods are received and then filed under order numbers.

In some cases perishable food items or certain other orders are placed over phone. It is not possible to send a purchase order to supplier by the purchase department in advance. The telephonic confirmation order should be sent off to the supplier as soon as possible. This order is quite similar to the purchase order but is also marked as 'Telephone Confirmation Order'. The receiving clerk compares the purchase order with delivery notes / supply order received along with the goods.

RECORDS MAINTAINED IN THE RECEIVING DEPARTMENT

The primary task of receiving department is to ensure that the hotel is receiving the correct quality and quantity of articles and the articles supplied as per the purchase order specifications not only in quantity but also in quality and the price charged is also as per the contracted rate.

The job of the receiving department is very technical and he is supposed to have a complete knowledge about each item's standard specifications.

- He must ensure that the tinned food supplied is fresh.
- The packaging is of right standard and is not damaged during transportation.
- In case of fresh fruits, vegetables, frozen food, etc. he should ensure that the items supplied are as per the standard specifications mentioned in the purchase order.
- If desired he can take the help of Chef in order to check the quality of the raw material.
- He should weight and count the items before receiving them.
- The Receiving officer should be suitably awarded through remuneration as otherwise, he will be tempted to receive variety of offers to receive goods of an inferior quality or short in quantity.
- The receiving department should be located in such a position that the goods may be quickly off loaded, checked/inspected, received and then easily distributed to the various stores, cellars, kitchens and other departments.

The area provided for receiving department should be large enough to handle the large quantity of goods and it should be easily cleanable and washable. It should be also very well lit and as far as possible it must have the natural light coming during day time. This department should have weighing scales to weight all kinds of goods. The ramp should be made so that the goods can be carried through trolley and if the store! On different floor level then goods lift/elevator should be available nearby to carry the goods.

RECEIVING PROCEDURE

The receiving department must have purchase order's copies along with the purchase specifications along with the delivery date and time and the supplier's name and details.

The following procedure is followed by the goods receiver after the goods are received at receiving department.

DELIVERY NOTE

The receiver checks the **delivery note** (supply note / order which comes along with the goods) and the copy of the purchase order along with purchase specification to ensure that the goods are received late then they are not accepted. For example 1000 kilogram of chicken is required for a party to commence at 6 p.m. and the supply of chicken comes at 4 p.m.: this supply should have supplied in right quantity, right quality and right time.

QUALITY

The quality supplied should be as per the purchase specification. In case of Branded products, the goods supplied should be of the same brand. For example if the purchase orders for 'Kisan Tomato Ketchup' of one kilogram size then the supply should be of the same brand and size.

THE INVOICE

Every time food is delivered to an establishment, it should be accompanied by a document that lists the items being delivered. For food, the document is normally an **invoice**, which is the same as a bill.

An **invoice** is usually presented to the receiving clerk in duplicate by the person making the delivery, who will expect the receiving clerk to sign and return the second copy. This serves as an acknowledgment to the purveyor that the establishment has received the products listed on the invoice.

BLIND RECEIVING

The copy of purchase order supplied to the receiving department does not show the quantity ordered. The invoices, delivery notes are sending to the accounts office directly. The receiving department has no other option then to count each and every item physically and receive the exact quantity / weight counted by him. The **Blind receiving** is giving the better receiving results and the efficiency of the receiving department can be easily evaluated.

PROCEDURES AND FORMS USED IN RECEIVING

The following forms are used during the receiving process:

- Purchase Orders
- Delivery Notes

1. PURCHASE ORDERS

Purchase officer places the purchase order with the suppliers giving details of the quantity and quality of items required to be delivered. The **purchase orders** are made out with five copies, each copy being colour coded to aid the correct distribution of them. The colour coding may differ from organization to organization.

i) White Copy (original)	sent to Supplier
ii) Yellow copy	sent to accounts department
iii) Green copy	sent to receiving department
iv) Pink copy	retained by the purchasing department
v) Off white copy	retained in the purchasing office and kept in date order wise and retained til the goods are received and then filled under order numbers.

2. DELIVERY NOTES

Delivery note comes along with each supply and this delivery note is sent by the supplier. The delivery note is compared with the purchase order for the quantity ordered. The delivery note is usually in duplicate.Goods received are as per the purchase order and delivery note then the original copy of the delivery note is retained by the receiving department and the duplicate copy is signed by the receiving department's official and send back to supplier through delivery man. In case the goods supplied are not as per specifications or the goods supplied are less then ordered then credit note is prepared and is signed by the delivery man. A copy of the credit note is sent to supplier through delivery man, a copy is send to purchase department, accounts department, control department and a copy is also retained by the receiving department.

EQUIPMENT REQUIRED BY RECEIVING DEPARTMENT

1. The equipment required by the receiving department can be broadly divided into major equipment and minor equipment. The receiving department should be well equipped with the various equipments so that the goods can be received efficiently made both the quantity as well as quality can be inspected.
2. The best way to minimize the opportunity to commit fraud is to implement a good system of internal controls. The three primary objectives of internal controls are to:

i. Promote operational efficiency;
ii. Ensure the accuracy and timeliness of financial information; and
iii. Encourage compliance with organizational policies, procedures, laws, and regulations.

An adequate internal control system should include the following four procedures:

1. PROPER AUTHORIZATION AND SEGREGATION OF DUTIES

The same employee should not perform more than one of the following job functions: authorization, execution, custody, and recording. The authorization function requires one employee to direct another employee to initiate and execute a transaction. The purchasing department then executes the transaction by placing an order for the requested materials with an approved vendor; a copy of the purchase order should go to the accounts payable and receiving departments. The items are delivered to the receiving department (a custody function), which, after verifying that the items had been ordered, should document their receipt and forward copies of the receiving documents to the accounts payable and purchasing departments. The vendor's invoice is sent to the accounts payable department, which, after verifying that the invoiced items have been ordered and received, prepares a check and then adjusts the accounts payable records accordingly (a recording function). Finally, an authorized check-signer should review supporting documentation (e.g., a purchase order, receiving report, and vendor invoice) to make sure that paid invoices are for items that have been ordered and received. Once the authorized check-signer is satisfied that the supporting documentation is in order, she should both sign the check and control the mailing (a custody function).

An employee who possesses two or more of these functions has what are commonly called incompatible responsibilities or inadequate segregation of duties. Such a situation can provide employees with the opportunity to commit fraud.

Consider the following case study of John, a long-time project manager for ABC, a medium-sized construction company. John had the responsibility to initiate purchase orders, an authorization function. Because materials were delivered directly to the job sites, John also verified that the materials had been received, custody functions. John had incompatible responsibilities that provided him with an opportunity to commit fraud that he then exploited. John simply created a fictitious (or shell) company called Specialty Supply Company. He then created bogus purchase orders (an authorization function) that were sent to a post office box John had set up for Specialty Supply Company. Using an Excel-generated invoice template, John then created bogus invoices and submitted them to ABC for payment.

John initialed the vendor invoices (a custody function) to confirm that the items had been received. A check was then prepared, signed, and mailed. John created a bank account in his own name doing business as Specialty Supply Company. John handwrote "Specialty Supply Company" on the backs of the vendor checks then deposited them into the account. Over a three-year period, John stole $100, 000 in this manner, and would have stolen more had the fraud not been detected through a tip from John's wife.

John's fraud could have been prevented by adequately segregating the job functions of authorization, execution, custody, and recording. Of course, employees possessing different functions can conspire together, but such situations are not the norm (80% of all frauds involve one person acting alone). Thus, the risk of fraud could be greatly reduced by adequately segregating job functions and making it very difficult for one person acting alone to perpetrate fraud.

2. ADEQUATE DOCUMENTS AND RECORDS

Documentation and records provide a paper trail that helps the company keep track of its assets, liabilities, and owners' equity. Companies with poor systems for tracking their resources tend to be breeding grounds for fraud. Understandably, employees are less inclined to steal if evidence of the theft is readily available in the company's documents and records.

3. PHYSICAL SAFEGUARDS

Companies should protect physical assets and accounting records by limiting access by unauthorized personnel. Such safeguards include cash registers, locked storerooms, passwords, fireproof safes, and fences around storage lots. Properly implemented, these safeguards minimize the opportunity for misuse or theft of the company's assets.

4. INDEPENDENT CHECKS

The notion underlying independent checks is that if employees know that their activities are being checked by others, the perceived opportunity to perpetrate fraud is reduced. For example, when an independent person (i.e., not a cashier) at a retail store compares the cash register tapes to the cash in the register and bank deposits, the manager is making sure that all cash rung into the cash register was deposited in the bank. Such independent checks not only guard against employee fraud but also uncover honest mistakes.

Few employees that steal expect to be caught and punished. Thus, an effective way to prevent fraud is to make employees think they will be caught and punished if they steal. Instilling this "perception of detection" in employees' minds is the single most effective way to prevent fraudulent activity. Implementing and adhering to a good system of internal controls helps protect profits from fraud

In this method there is no invoice accompanying the delivery.The purveyors prepare regular invoice but they mail them directly to the hotel accounting office.The list will accompany the actual order; it may also indicate the totals.The receiving clerk has to make a complete listngs of each item by counting or weighing and recording every article.This method forces the receiving clerk to do the job very carefully. He cannot arbitrarily sign an invoice without actually inspecting the merchandise.He does not have an invoice, he has to write himself, he has to count and weight each item and wrote it down.

The receiving clerk sends the finished record to the accounting office. The accounting personnel compare the receiving clerk records with the invoice that is received in the mail from the purveyor. The accounting office should also check price and extensions as is done in a standard receiving routine.

- Store will receive the goods blind and reweight the goods received.
- Dtails of goods received in stores will be entered by the storekeeper on "Receiving Returns" in triplicate.
- All three copies on the receiving returns will be then be handled over the accounting department representative at stores who will use those to fill in the store record cards. Kardex cards for each items will have the relevant material code.He will then fill in the following columns in the receiving returns:
    - Purchase order number and date
    - The second copy of the receiving return will be retained and filled in stores.
- The original and first copy of the form will be sent to accounting department.
- Accounting office with then compare items and quantities on the day receiving return with those on the daily receiving report received from receiving section to ensure that these agrees
- The accounting department will finally complete the original first copy of the receiving return by filling in the following columns:
    - Date of bill passing

- Voucher number
- VALUE OF RECIPT

- The original will be filed month by month in the accounting department.
- The first copy of the receiving return will be retained by accounting department who will file them with the relevant vouchers for payments to supplier.

ADVANTAGES

- It is an excellent method.
- It gives the best possible control.

DISADVANTAGES

- It is an expensive and time consuming procedure.It takes a lot of time for receiving clerk to get and record all information involved.In the accounting department also it takes a lot of time.

FRAUDS IN THE RECEIVING DEPARTMENT

The internal control system is not only designed to prevent and detect fraud, but also to prevent and detect error which is usually more common that fraud. Though it is very difficult to list down all types of frauds, in fact every moment some where in the world, a new type of fraud takes place. Some of the common frauds are as follows:

- Failure to make check
- Failure to record sales summary sheet
- Under recording of sale
- Picking up of food without proper check
- Collecting payment from guest without check
- Charging incorrect room rent
- Selling room without registration
- Payment of bill twice
- Receiving the bill without goods
- Receiving bills twice for one supply
- Receiving goods and bills without any purchase order
- Allowance or discount allowed without proper authorization
- Ghost pay rolls
- Full payment made for substandard goods received
- Stealing hotels inventory and assets

HYGIENE AND CLEANINESS OF THE RECEVING AREA

Several methods should be adopted to ensure the proper cleaniness and hygiene of the receeving area.proper cleaniness of the receiving area identifies the proper safety and cleaniness of the food materials. The cleaniness of the receiving area is necessary as it is very important for the premises to have a proper safety of the materials being received and to store them safey so that they are not easily being damaged.

Some of the common steps for hygiene and cleaniness of the receiving area are as follows:

1. Proper storage space is required so that it is easy to store the receivable materials.
2. Proper brooming of the receiving area at regular intervals.
3. Wipe down the outside of the vent hood.Use a soapy cloth to clean the outside of the vent hood
4. Clean out your cabinets.Whether they contain food, kitchen supllies, or your seceret stash of candy, you should clean your cabinets out every once in a while.
5. Wipe down your counters with cleaning supplies
6. Keep the garbage disposal working properly
7. Sweep and mop your floor when necessary
8. Put all the things back to their place after there use so that the things do not get mixed up.
9. Take out the trash at the end of the day
10. Always wear gloves while receiving the food articles.
11. The storage area should be always kept clean.
12. The food articles should be kept seperately. I.e. the meat and the meat products should be kept separate whereas the veg articles should have a separate place.
13. Always check the expiry date before receiving the article.
14. Periodic cleaning of the freezer and the deep freezer.

QUESTIONNAIRE

1. Write notes on:
   i. Blind receiving
   ii. Credit note
   iii. Delivery note

iv. Meat tag
v. Blind receiving
vi. Good received book
vii. Daily receiving report
viii. Receiving procedure

2. From the following invoice the food purchases made on 10th June prepare the receivers report for the same day:

Company	*Item*	*Total Amount*	*Distribution*
James and Co.	Fresh Meat	Rs. 8, 430.20	to kitchen
Baker & Co.	Baked goods	Rs. 1510.20	to kitchen
Sole & Co.	Fish	Rs. 2190.40	Fresh
MacDonalds	Canned Fruits	Rs. 7144.50	to store
Vally Dairy	Dairy Products	Rs. 1844.00	to kitchen

3. Define Receiving. Explain the purchase procedure in a five star hotel.
4. What is receiving control?
5. What are the aims and objectives of receiving control?
6. What points you have to consider while receiving food?
7. What is blind receiving?
8. What are the receiving procedures and controls?
9. Explain the job description of receving clerk/personnel?
10. What is the equipment required during receiving?
11. Explain the fraud in receiving control.
12. Explain the hygeine and cleanliness procedure of cost.

UNIT 4

STORING AND ISSUING CONTROL

A. STORING CONTROL

Define as the process of establishing standard and procedure for storing.

The term store, storehouse, or Warehouse refers to a building where materials are kept.

An organisation has various types of sores as raw material store, where goods kept in huge shelves.

The basic motive of the Store department is to supply the requisite stores to kitchen, restaurants, bars, housekeeping etc. as & when required. The should be no wastage of stores due to bad storage, overstocking, wrong storing, wrong issuing (FIFO) etc.

B. AIMS OF STORE CONTROL

1. To provide Maintenance material, Spare Parts and general store as required.
2. To receive and Dispatch finished Goods.
3. To make available and balanced flow of Raw Material.
4. To make a proper control over Threads
5. Proper Inventory of store ensuring adequate staff in Hand.
6. To accept and store scrap and other discard material as they arise and also arrange for Disposal.

C. JOB DESCRIPTION OF FOOD STORE ROOM PERSONNEL

Reports to: **Store Supervisor**

- Keeping proper record of transactions made for receiving & issuing of goods.

- Ensure proper storing of goods.
- Ensure proper supply of goods receiving.
- Assign location for storage of different commodities as perishable & non-perishable items.
- Identification of all material stored.
- Receipt of incoming material.
- Inspection of all receipt from renders & sub contractors.
- Storage & preservation.
- Material handling & packing.
- Processing of customer orders.
- Dispatch of finished goods.
- Issue of material to users within the organization.
- Maintenance of stock records.
- Store accounting.
- Inventory control.

D. CONDITIONS OF FACILITIES & EQUIPMENT

The factors involved in maintaining proper internal conditions include temperature, storage containers, shelving, and cleanliness. Problems with any or all of these may lead to spoilage and waste. It should be noted that all states and many municipalities have sanitation and health codes that must be followed by all foodservice facilities. These codes specify storage temperatures, storage containers, and storage procedures, among many other requirements such as hot water temperatures, sanitation requirements, and so on. Inspectors regularly visit establishments and grade them on their adherence to the codes. It is thus imperative that foodservice employees have a detailed knowledge of sanitation and health codes for their particular areas.

TEMPERATURE

One of the key factors in storing foods is the temperature of the storage facility. This is particularly important for perishables. Food life can be maximized when food is stored at the correct temperature and at the proper level of humidity. The food controller should occasionally check the temperature gauges on the refrigerated storage facilities to see that the appropriate temperatures are being maintained. The temperatures that follow are generally accepted as optimum for storing the foods indicated:

Fresh Meats	34 F to 36 F
Fresh Diary	34 F to 36 F
Fresh Fish	30 F to 34 F
Frozen Food	-10 F to 0 F

TEMPERATURE OF BEVERAGES

Red Wines	13-16 °C (55-60)F
Sparkling Wines	13 °C (55 F)
White Wines	10 °C (50 F)
Fortified Wines	17-22 °C
Soft Drinks	13 °C (55 F)
Beer	13 °C (55 F)
Spirits	13-16 °C (55-60)F

If temperatures are permitted to rise above these levels, shelf life is shortened and the risk of food spoilage is increased for perishables. Proper temperature can also be a key factor in preventing spoilage of non perishables. Storage facilities for staple food products should usually be room temperature, approximately 65 to 70 degrees F. Sometimes, particularly in older establishments, staples are kept in facilities that are either too warm because of their proximity to hot stoves or steam pipes running through the ceiling, or too cold because they are located in unheated parts of a building. Although the degree of risk is not as great with staples, it should be remembered that all foods are ultimately perishable and that the shelf life of food is increased by storage at proper temperatures.

STORAGE CONTAINERS

In addition to maintaining foods at proper temperatures, care must be given to storing them in appropriate containers. Many staples are purchased in airtight containers, but offers are purchased in unsealed containers—paper bags, boxes, and sacks—which are susceptible to attack by insects and vermin. Whenever practicable, products purchased in unsealed packages should be transferred to tight, insect proof containers. In the case of perishables, both raw and cooked, care should be given to storing them in whatever manner will best maintain their original quality. Many raw foods, such as apples and potatoes, may be stored as purchased for reasonable periods; others, such as fresh fish, should be packed in shaved ice. In general, cooked foods and opened canned foods should be stored in stainless steel containers, either wrapped or appropriately covered.

• **SHELVING**

For perishable foods, shelving should be slatted to permit maximum circulation of air in refrigerated facilities. For non perishables, solid steel shelving is usually preferred. At no time should any food product be stored on the floor. Appropriate shelving raised a few inches above the floor level should be provided for larger and heavier containers.

- There are a wide variety of shelf options available. Determine the amount you feel comfortable spending and consider what will suit your needs best.
- Options for canned goods and other Three Month Supply foods:
    - **Inexpensive metal or plastic shelving** (i.e. from Walmart) – A cheap and easy way to get started, shelves may not be as durable. Be careful with cheaper metal shelves as they may bow in the middle.

- **Higher quality metal shelves** – Heavy duty hardware store shelves should have no problem with bowing or collapsing under heavy food weights.
- **Deluxe Can Rotation System** – Most expensive option, but very convenient for easily rotating through foods.

CLEANLINESS

Absolute cleanliness is a condition that should be enforced in all food storage facilities at all times. In refrigerated facilities, this will prevent the accumulation of small amounts of spoiling food, which can give off odours and may affect other foods. In storeroom facilities, it will discourage infestation by insects and vermin. Storerooms should be swept and cleaned daily, and no clutter should be allowed to accumulate. A professional examiner should be brought in on a regular basis to prevent rodents and vermin from reaching population levels large enough to cause damage and disease.

E. ARRANGEMENTS OF FOOD

The factors involved in maintaining an appropriate internal arrangement of foods include keeping the most-used items readily available, fixing definite locations for each item, and rotating stock.

KEEPING THE MOST-USED ITEMS READILY AVAILABLE

It is usually helpful to arrange storage facilities so that the most frequently used items are kept closest to the entrance. Although it has no effect on spoilage or theft, this arrangement does tend to reduce the time required to move needed foods from storage to production and thus tends to reduce labour costs.

FIXING DEFINITE LOCATION

Each particular item should always be found in the same location, and attention should be given to ensuring that new deliveries of the item are stored in the same location. All too often, one product is stored in several locations at once (for example, six cans on a shelf and two partially used cases in two other areas). This increases the chances for over purchasing, spoilage, and theft. In addition, it makes difficult the monthly process of taking a physical inventory. Incidentally, separate facilities for storage of different classes of foods should be maintained whenever practicable and possible. Eggs, for example, should not be stored with fish, cheese, or other foods that give off odours, because their shells are quite porous and they will absorb flavours from other foods. Fish should always be stored in separate facilities.

ROTATION OF STOCK

The food controller must establish procedures to ensure that older quantities of any item are used before any new deliveries. The procedure used to do this is known as the first-in, first-out method of stock rotation, commonly called FIFO in the industry. The steward and staff must be held responsible for storing new deliveries of an item behind the quantities already on hand, thus ensuring that older items will be used first. This reduces the possibilities for spoilage. If this procedure is not followed and those who store foods are permitted to put new food in front of old food on shelves, the chances are increased that the older items will spoil before they are used. Ensuring that stock rotation takes place is particularly important with perishables, but it should not be neglected with non perishables.

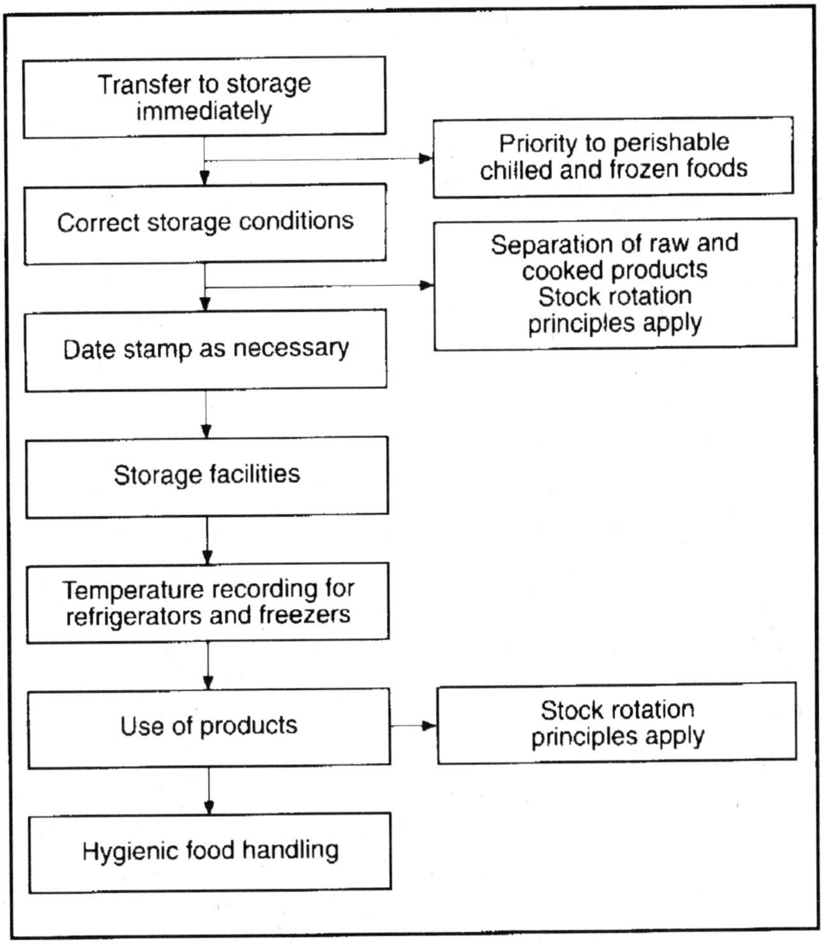

F. LOCATION OF STORAGE FACILITIES

Whenever possible, the storage facilities for both perishable and non-perishable foods should be located between receiving areas and preparation areas, preferably close to both. Such locations facilitate the moving of foods from the receiving areas to storage and from storage to the preparation areas. A properly located storage facility will have the effect of:

1. Speeding the Storing & Issuing of Food.
2. Maximizing Security.
3. Reducing Labour Requirements.

G. SECURITY

Food should never be stored in a manner that permits pilferage. That is another reason for moving foods from the receiving area to storage as quickly as possible. Once in storage, appropriate security must be maintained at all times. A store room for staple food products should never be left open and unattended. Employees should not be permitted to remove items at will. Typically, a storeroom is kept open at specified times for specified periods well known to the staff and is otherwise closed to enable the storeroom clerk to attend to other duties. When the storeroom is closed, it should be locked, and the single key should be in the storeroom clerk's possession. In such cases, one additional "emergency" key is usually kept by the manager or in the office safe. Security is also an important consideration in storing perishables, particularly in the case of high-cost items such as meat and fish. The importance of security obviously increases with the value of the items stored. It is sometimes advisable to establish separate control procedures for steaks, liquor, and other high-cost items.

H. STOCK CONTROL

Stock control is used to show how much stock you have at a point in time, and how you keep track of it.

It applies to every item you use to produce from raw materials to finished goods and whether it is a product or service. It covers stock at each stage of the production process, from purchase and delivery to using and re-ordering the stock.

Having the right amount of stock is important as it ensures that capital is not tied up unnecessarily, and protects production if problems arise with the supply chain.

STOCK BOOK REGISTER

		Date			Date			Date		
Date	Particulars	Receipt	Issue	Balance	Receipt	Issue	Balance	Receipt	Issue	Balance

I. TWO TYPES OF FOODS RECEIVED

DIRECT

Directs are charged to food cost as they are received, on the assumption that these perishable items have been purchased for immediate use. Theoretically, these foods will be moved to appropriate facilities in or near the kitchen and will be used entirely in food preparation on the day they are received. In practice, this is not normally the case. Some of the directs received on a given day are likely to be left over and used the following day; in fact, most establishments purposely purchase more than one day's supply of many directs. Although this greatly simplifies the record keeping associated with determining the cost of directs, it does introduce some inaccuracy in the records maintained. Establishments that determine daily food costs use the total dollar figure in the "Food Direct" column on the Receiving Clerk's Daily Report as one component of the daily cost of food. This is based on the presumption that all directs received on a given day have been consumed and should thus be included in food cost for that day. Because this is not strictly true, these daily costs tend to be artificially high on days when all directs received have not been consumed and artificially low on days when directs included in costs for previous days are actually being consumed. For record-keeping purposes, then, directs are treated as issued the moment they are received, and no further record of particular items is kept.

STORES

The food category known as stores was previously described as consisting of (1) staples and (2) tagged items, primarily meats. When purchased, these foods are considered part of inventory until issued for use and are not included in cost figures until they are issued. Therefore, it follows that records of issues must be kept in order to determine the cost of stores. For control purposes, a system must be established to ensure that no stores are issued unless kitchen personnel submit lists of the items and quantities needed.

J. STOCK RECORDS MAINTAINED BIN CARDS

Bin Cards are prepared for each item stored in the store. It contains the description of the item, balance of the item, quantity of goods received; the quantity of goods issued and the balance of the item are shown on daily basis. It also shows the minimum stock, reordering point / level, maximum stock, danger point / level economic ordering quantity. The bin cards are either kept along with each item or they are stored near the store keeper working table.

A SPECIMEN BIN CARD

BIN CARD

Maximum stock level :........................ Material Code:..................
Minimum stock level: ....
BC No: ....
Order Level: .... Description:.......................

RECEIPTS			ISSUES			BALANCE		AUDIT
Date	GRN No.	Quant.	Date	MFR No.	Quant.	Quant.	Date	Initials

K. ISSUING CONTROL

Directs were defined as those foods charged to cost as purchased & stores as those carried in inventory & charged to cost as issued. From the point of view of a food controller, that distinction becomes particularly important in a discussion of issuing procedures. Its importance will become increasingly apparent as we approach the disunion of the calculation of food cost.

L. REQUISITIONS

A requisition, illustrated in a table is a form prepared by a member of the kitchen shaft listing the items & quantities needed from stores is should be received by chef, who should check to see that each item appearing is genuinely required in the amount listed. The requisition is then approved & signed by the chef. This has the desirable effect of forcing kitchen personnel to anticipate needs &plan for the following day's production.

REQUISITION AND ISSUE VOUCHER

Requisition and Issue Voucher No.: ____________________

Date: ______________ Ship to: ____________________

____

____

REQUISITION			ISSUE		Remarks
Article	Quantity on Hand	Quantity Requested	Shipped	Received	

REQUISITION
Requested by: ____________________ Date: ________

Approved by: ____________________ Date: ________

ISSUE:
Approved by: ____________________ Date: ________

Shipped by: ____________________ Date: ________

RECEIPT:
Received by: ____________________ Date: ________

(make 4 copies)

It is also desirable in many instances, to set defined times for the issuing of food by the storekeeper, who, after all, has a number of other duties to perform, including keeping the store rooms and refrigerators clean, maintaining stokes of samples on shelves, rotating stock, & doing considerable paper work. Some operations have achieved good results by restricting the items for issuing food two hours in the morning and two hours in the afternoon. Naturally, such decision must be left to management in any particular operation.

M. TRANSFER NOTES

Transfer of food items both in the raw form or cooked / semi-cooked form from one department to another department within the hotel is done through transfer notes. For example, the kitchen may make out a transfer note to the room service bar for Irish Whisky for making an Irish coffee. Usually bar makes its own requisition for fresh fruits and picks them up from stores. But at times the bar may make a transfer note for fresh fruits like oranges, pineapple, lemons, etc. and pick them up from kitchen. The columns of the transfer form may be quite similar to the requisition form. Both transfer notes and requisition slips are internal invoices.

All requisition slips and transfer notes are sent to control department and accounts department for control and accounting purpose.

INTRA UNIT TRANSFER

Food and beverage transfer

We assume that a restaurant purchases, receives, stores, and issues food for use in one kitchen in which all production is accomplished. By doing so, we have quite purposely ignored the existence of a number of possible complications, which will be useful to consider at this point. For example, even in small restaurants, food production in the kitchen may require the use of certain beverage items, such as wines and liquors, not purchased specifically for kitchen use. Conversely, many establishments purchase some food items, knowing that they will be used at the bar for drink production. Whole oranges and lemons, as well as heavy cream, are good examples. In addition, in some large hotel and motel operations, more than one kitchen is in operation and it may be necessary or desirable to transfer food from one kitchen to another.

Transfers may occur in chain operations: A single unit may produce such items as baked goods for other units in the chain, or one unit in the organization, running short of needed items, may be encouraged to secure them from another unit. In these cases, a failure to record the value of transfers will result in a food cost that is inaccurate.

Because the goals of food control include determining food cost as accurately as possible and matching food cost with food sales, it is often necessary to maintain records of the cost of the food transferred. When the amounts involved are relatively insignificant and have little appreciable effect on cost and on the cost-to-sales ratio, they may be and usually are disregarded. But when the amounts become somewhat larger and have more significant effects, records of some type must be developed.

INTRA-UNIT TRANSFERS

Intraunit transfers are food and beverage transfers between departments of a food and beverage operation. They include transfers of food and liquor between the kitchen and bar, and between kitchen and kitchen in those larger operations that have multiple feeding facilities.

Between Kitchen and Kitchen (intraunit)

In some of the larger hotels that operate more than one kitchen and dining room, it is common practice to determine food costs for each separately and to match the costs for each operating unit with the sales generated by that unit. When some food items are transferred from one kitchen to another, higher degrees of accuracy in determining food costs may be achieved by keeping records of items and amounts so transferred. In cases where, for example, one unit closes earlier than another and cooked foods may be conveniently transferred from the closing unit to the one remaining open until a later hour, it may be possible to achieve a higher degree of accuracy in determining costs for each unit by crediting the cost of the early closing unit for the value of the items transferred and by adding that value to the cost for the later-closing unit.

Reg No.	ITEM	SIZE	QUANTITY TRANSFERRED	COST
Requested By:	Delivered By:	Received By:	Cost Controller:	

SAMPLE BUTCHER SHOP TRANSFER

ABC HOTEL LTD. No...........

Department......... Dated..........

Even in cases in which items are not so transferred but are merely returned to a central kitchen or commissary for reissue to the same or to other units on succeeding days, recording the value of the items returned on transfer memos or on similar forms makes possible a more accurate determination of food costs and, consequently, of cost-to-sales ratios for operating periods.

Interunit Transfers

Interunit transfers are transfers of food and beverage between units in a chain. The two examples that follow illustrate interunit transfers and the effect of such transfers on food costs. In a number of instances, small chains produce some items (baked goods, for example) in only one unit and then distribute those items to other units in the chain. If the ingredients for the baked goods come from that particular unit's regular supplies, then some record must be made of the cost of the ingredients used. Failure to record such costs can result in overstating the food cost of the producing unit by the value of the ingredients used, and in understating the food costs of the receiving units by the value of the foods they receive.

In addition, if the matching principle as discussed below is to be followed and if food sales are reported separately for each unit, then food cost figures that do not include the cost of all those foods sold, including the baked goods from another unit, cannot be said to be truly matched with sales. Under such conditions, if one of management's goals is to match costs and sales with a reasonably high degree of accuracy, it is necessary to use a transfer memo or a similar form to record the value of ingredients used to produce finished products to be transferred to other units. With such records available, it is possible to decrease the cost of the producing unit by the amount transferred. Appropriately increasing the food cost figures of the receiving units may pose more of a problem.

If each unit receives an equal share of the goods produced, then one could simply divide the cost of the goods produced and credited to the producing unit by the number of units to which items have been transferred, and then increase the food cost of each by one equal share. However, if the total produced for distribution to the various units is not divided among them equally, then some more equitable means for apportioning cost must be found.

Another problem involving the value of foods transferred from one unit to another may be seen in those chain organizations that permit or encourage unit managers to obtain foods from other units when their own supplies run low and additional purchases are precluded by lack of time. Occasions may arise when a unit nearly exhausts the supply of an important item and does not discover this shortage until it is clearly too late to purchase an additional amount. In some organizations, when units are comparatively close to one another and offer identical menus, items are borrowed and returned within a day or so as a matter of course, and no complications arise as long as all borrowed items are returned. However, not all cases are quite so simple, as, for example, when a perishable item borrowed by one unit does not appear on the menu again for some considerable period of time. Rather than maintain records over long periods to ensure the return of borrowed items, it is often simpler to record such transfers of foods on transfer memos and to use the information so recorded to increase the cost of the unit that has borrowed and correspondingly decrease the cost of the supplying unit.

An interesting problem that may arise in connection with this procedure is the extent to which it influences some managers to purposely maintain short supplies of some high-cost and perishable items. If the organization permits one unit to secure needed supplies from other units at the same prices it would pay in the market, some managers will be encouraged to reduce the possibilities for excessive costs due to spoilage and pilferage in their units simply by maintaining inadequate supplies. Under such conditions, discouraging managers from taking advantage may entail establishing a price for transfer purposes somewhat higher than the current market price.

Between Bar and Kitchen (inter unit)

Food and beverage transfers between bar and kitchen occur frequently in operations of all sizes. Many kitchens use beverage items such as wine, cordials, brandy, and even ale to produce sauces, parfaits, certain baked items, and rarebits. Occasionally, these beverages are purchased by the food department for use in the kitchen, kept in a storeroom until needed, and then issued on requisitions directly to the kitchen. In such cases, additional records are not required; the quantities and values listed on the requisition are sufficient to permit accurate calculations of cost. However, in most instances when these beverages are needed in the kitchen, appropriate amounts are obtained from the bar. After all, if sufficient supplies are already being maintained at the bar, it makes little sense to keep additional quantities for specific use in food production.

The same may be said of certain food items in the directs category used by bartenders in drink production. If supplies of oranges, lemons, limes, heavy cream, and eggs are already available in a kitchen, it makes little sense to purchase specific supplies of these items for exclusive use at the bar. It is far simpler merely to secure the needed items from the kitchen. When it becomes necessary or desirable to achieve a high degree of accuracy in determining costs to match with sales, records of these transfers between the food and beverage departments must be maintained.

The form used to maintain these records is the Food/Beverage Transfer Memo. As transfers are made, items and amounts are recorded. These records are sent to the food controller, who can use them to adjust food cost figures to achieve greater accuracy, and then routed to the food controller and an accounting office, where the appropriate adjusting entries can be made in the financial records.

N. PERPETUAL INVENTORY METHOD

Perpetual Inventory means checking of stock items from one day to another. The control department maintains the inventory control card / record for each item held in stores. **Perpetual inventory** or **continuous inventory** describes systems of inventory where information on inventory quantity and availability is updated on a continuous basis as a function of doing business. Generally this is accomplished by connecting the inventory system with order entry and in retail the point of sale system. In this case, book inventory would be exactly the same as, or almost the same, as the real inventory.

In earlier periods, non-continuous or periodic inventory systems were more prevalent. Starting in the 1970s digital computers made possible the ability to implement a perpetual inventory system. This has been facilitated by bar coding and lately radio frequency identification labeling which allows computer systems to quickly read and process inventory information as part of transaction processing.

Perpetual inventory systems can still be vulnerable to errors due to overstatements (phantom inventory) or understatements (missing inventory) that can occur as a result of theft, breakage, scanning errors or untracked inventory movements, leading to systematic errors in replenishment

All commodities received and issued are recorded date wise. The goods are received by the receiving department as per the purchase order, supply order, invoice and records the goods received in the goods received register. He transfers the goods received to stores. The store department enters the goods received in its records and also records them on all bin cards and stock cards. If the records are maintained properly by stores, receiving department then it becomes very easy to check it at any time for accuracy of entries and for control purposes.

PERPETUAL INVENTORY CARD

ABC HOTELS LTD.

PERPETUAL INVENTORY CARD

ITEM...... COST......
SIZE....... PARSTOCK.........
SUPPLIER......... RECORDER POINT......
....
....

DATE	ORDER NO.	IN	OUT	BALANCE
....	....	....	......	....
....	....	....	......	....
....	....	....	......	....
....	....	....	......	....
....	....	....	......	....
....	....	....	......	....
....	....	....	......	....

O. MONTHLY INVENTORY/ STOCK TAKING

In most business establishment, including food & beverage operations, one universally accepted practice is the taking of a physical inventory. It done at the close of an accounting period, typically after the close of business on the last day of a calendar month. In our discussion here we will be concerned only with those dealing in food & beverage items purchased primarily for the purpose of making and selling food & beverage products.

The regular and surprise stock taking is must for an effective control. This should be followed in addition to daily check kept on the receipt and issue of items from 3 stores. The stock variation may not be always due to pilferage but usually the variation in physical stock as compare the stock as per Bin card may be due to variation in weighing (short weighing or over weighing). In case of a little bit variation, the store keeper may be warned orally to be more careful; n weighing the items while issuing.

The purpose of beverage stock taking is to ascertain the actual value of beverages in stores and much it is different from book value. Usually every day after the bar is closed the physical stock taking of all beverages is taken. The Open spirits are measured physically to know the exact number of drinks in stock. The balance c/f becomes the balance b/d en the following day.

All purchases / requisitions are added and the balance shown at the end of the shift is deducted to know the actual consumption for the day. The daily stock taking is usually done by the representative from the control department. The bar man is required to assist in the stock taking.

The following are the reasons for stock taking:

1. **Stock in Hand:**

   To calculate the profit and loss account, it is must to know the actual value of stock in Rupees to show it as a stock in the books. The stock of items is taken physically and the value of the stock in hand is calculated Usually the actually cost or the current market price, whichever is lower is taken into account for calculation the value of stock.

2. **Discrepancy:**

   No matter how carefully the receipts and issue of goods are recorded in the stores records but still there might be discrepancy in the physical stock in hand as compare to the stock in books. Management must ensure that these discrepancies must be minimised if not eliminated all together.

3. **Printed Stock Sheets:**

   The stock taking should be taken by the group of persons consisting of officials from Control department Accounts department and Food and Beverage department. The printed stock sheets are prepared as this helps in taking the stock more speedily.

4. **Time of Stock Taking:**

   Usually the stock taking is done either after the closing hour of the stores or before opening of the normal stores timings. This is done to avoide any disturbance to the routine distribution of the requisitions to various departments.

5. **Professional Stock Takers:**

   The management may hire professionals for Stock taking at least once month. This ensures that the stock taking is done more systematically efficiently by the internal staff of the hotel

P. PRICING OF COMMODITIES

All food items issued to departments should be fairly charged for calculating food cost. Food cost is a very vital tool of evaluating kitchens efficiency and management gives a lot of importance to the food cost.

The method of pricing the food issued depends on the type of commodity. The commodities can be broadly divided Into Perishables and Non-Perishables

PERISHABLES

Almost all perishable commodities directly go to the kitchen and are priced at actual purchase price. The perishables which first go to the stores and then issued daily basis to the kitchens against requisitions then are prices differently. The biggest problem of calculating cost is of meat and meat products. The animal carcass is issued to butcher against requisition. Butchery makes the appropriate portion sizes for different menu items as per the kitchens requirements. The butchery transfers the food to kitchens against transfer notes. The food items mentioned on the transfer notes and transferred from butchery and priced. While calculating the price of meat products the butchery keeps in mind the wastage and the actual yield is priced for control and costing purpose.

The procurement price of an item may or may not be same as purchase price. In case goods are purchased through agent or the supplier is quoting price ex-showroom / store then the hotel is required to pay the commission to the agent and carriage inward charges for transporting the goods to the hotel. For majority of the consumable items which are usually consumed with in a day or two of purchasing are usually charged on purchase price for calculating food cost.

NON-PERISHABLE

In case of non-perishable items there are several different methods to price the items/commodities. But only one of the methods is adopted to price the commodities.

The different prices are:

1. **Average Price:**

   In case the price of an item fluctuates very frequently and every time it is purchased the price may be different then the price paid, may be a day before. These items when issued to departments against requisitions are charged while calculating the average price paid for the item. This ensures more stability in the issue price of the commodities and hence does not affect adversely on the food cost.

2. **Weighted Average Price:**

   The weighted average of the items is calculated to have more stability in issue price as compare to Average Price. For example if 100 packets of mushrooms are purchased at the price of Rs. 8 per packet and 400 packets mushrooms are purchased at the price of Rs. 7. Then the Weighted Average Price will be 100 X 8 + 400 X 7 divided by 500= Rs. 7.20 per packet.

3. **LIFO: last in first out:**

   When the market fluctuates very frequently and the management wants to charge the latest price of the commodity even when the goods received first are issued first (FIFO). But in case latest price is less than the first price then the price paid for the commodities is charged to department issued stores.

4. **FIFO: first in first out:**

   This means the goods purchased first will be issued first and also the same price will be charged while issuing stores.

5. **Standard price:**

   Irrespective of the price paid for procuring the commodities but the price charged is fixed by the management. Usually the management fixes the price of a commodity for a certain period say three to six months and the same price is charged to departments while issuing commodities against requisition. This helps in maintaining the food cost irrespective of the market price.

Q. STOCK TAKING AND COMPARISON OF ACTUAL PHYSICAL INVENTORY AND BOOK VALUE

The regular and surprise stock taking is must for an effective control. This should be followed in addition to daily check kept on the receipt and issue of items from 3 stores. The stock variation may not be always due to pilferage but usually the variation in physical stock as compare the stock as per Bin card may be due to variation in weighing (short weighing or over weighing). In case of a little bit variation, the store keeper may be warned orally to be more careful in weighing the items while issuing.

The purpose of beverage stock taking is to ascertain the actual value of beverages in stores and much it is different from book value. Usually every day after the bar is closed the physical stock taking of all beverages is taken. The Open spirits are measured physically to know the exact number of drinks in stock. The balance c/f becomes the balance b/d en the following day.

All purchases/requisitions are added and the balance shown at the end of the shift is deducted to know the actual consumption for the day. The daily stock taking is usually done by the representative from the control department. The bar man is required to assist in the stock taking.

The following are the reasons for stock taking:

1. **Stock in Hand:**

   To calculate the profit and loss account, it is must to know the actual value of stock in Rupees to show it as a stock in the books. The stock of items is taken physically and the value of the stock in hand is calculated usually the actually cost or the current market price, whichever is lower is taken into account for calculation the value of stock.

2. **Discrepancy:**

   No matter how carefully the receipts and issue of goods are recorded in the stores records but still there might be discrepancy in the physical stock in hand as compare to the stock in books. Management must ensure that these discrepancies must be minimised if not eliminated all together.

2. **Printed Stock Sheets:**

   The stock taking should be taken by the group of persons consisting of officials from Control department Accounts department and Food and Beverage department. The printed stock sheets are prepared as this helps in taking the stock more speedily.

4. **Time of Stock Taking:**

   Usually the stock taking is done either after the closing hour of the stores or before opening of the normal stores timings. This is done to avoide any disturbance to the routine distribution of the requisitions to various departments.

5. **Professional Stock Takers:**

   The management may hire professionals for Stock taking at least once month. This ensures that the stock taking is done more systematically efficiently by the internal staff of the hotel.

R. STOCK LEVELS

The stock level has a direct impact on either running out of stock of an item or of over stocking of an item, and thereby tying up unnecessary working capital. The management would like to have a stock level which should neither have a stock level which should neither have a situation of running out of stock nor over stocking.

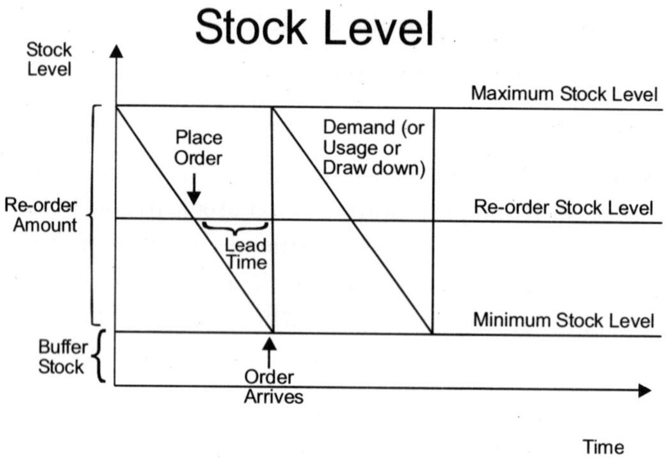

This stock level in any hotel may differ from hotel to hotel depending upon the following reason:

a) Forecast on volume of sales.
b) Reordering time for the item.
c) The economic ordering quantity.
d) Expected price of the item, availability, etc.
e) The storage space and facility available
f) The shelf life/keeping quality of the item.
g) Working capital available.
h) Danger level

S. HYGIENE & CLEANLINESS OF AREA

Absolute cleanliness is a condition that should be enforced in all food storage facilities at all times. In refrigerated facilities, this will prevent the accumulation of small amounts of spoiling food, which can give off odors and may affect other foods. In storeroom facilities, it will discourage infestation by insects and vermin. Storerooms should be swept and cleaned daily, and no clutter should be allowed to accumulate. A professional exterminator should be brought in on a regular basis to prevent rodents and vermin from reaching population levels large enough to cause damage and disease.

QUESTIONNAIRE

1. What is Storing Control & what are its aims? Also briefly explain the job description of Food Store Room Personnel?
2. What are the types of food received in Storing Control?
3. Draw the formats:
    1. Bin Cards
    2. Stock Book Register
    3. Requisition & Issue Voucher
    4. Transfer Notes
    5. Monthly Inventory
4. Differentiate between Interunit Transfer & Intraunit Transfer. Give an example of each in support of your answer?
5. Define Stock Taking & reasons for Stock Taking?
6. How pricing of Commodities are done?
7. Differentiate between Perishable & Non-Perishable Commodities?
8. Explain Stock Level with the help of a graph?
9. Write Short Notes on:
    1. Rotation of Stock
    2. Shelving
    3. Requisition
    4. LIFO
    5. FIFO
    6. Standard Price
    7. Transfer Notes
    8. Perpetual Inventory Method.
10. Explain the role of Hygiene & Cleanliness in Storing goods?

UNIT 5

PRODUCTION CONTROL

INTRODUCTION

Production is a process where raw material is converted into semi finished products and thereby adds to the value of utility of products, which can be measured as the difference between the value of inputs and value of outputs.

Production Control is a process that comprises the systematic planning, coordinating and directing of all manufacturing activities and influences to insure having goods made on time, of adequate, and at reasonable cost. It is a system with proper production planning.

- Aims and Objectives
- Forecasting
- Fixing of Standards
- Computation of Staff Meals

AIMS AND OBJECTIVES OF PRODUCTION CONTROL

1. To regulate and control the various operations of production process.
2. To facilitate food cost control for the establishment.
3. To reduce the wastage.
4. To reduce the problem of food that is left over and its reuse.
5. To facilitate the purchasing of food stuff, especially the perishable food items and ensure that proper stock level is maintained.
6. To eliminate the incorrect portion size.
7. To make available supply of raw material and equipments for the smooth functioning.

8. To ensure the right handling of raw material and product.
9. To reduce the over production waste during cooking, storing, purchasing, processing, portion size etc.
10. To predict the choice of menu items by customers.
11. To predict the total number of meals to be sold in each selling outlet of the hotel.

The following stages are used to control the production:

- Forecasting
- Standard Yields
- Standard Recipe
- Standard Portion Size
- Standard portion cost

VOLUME FORECASTING

Forecasting is a technique of predicting the volume of sales of food & beverage outlets in a specific period. It is a science of predicting future outcomes. It is a highly professional job and should be done by professionals only. It is not only the total volume of food and beverage sale but the forecasting is to be made for volume of individual items sale. This forecasting helps kitchen and management to prepare the food of such quantity that neither the food is wasted due to over production nor orders are refused due to under production. The forecasting can be done for the year, season, month, and week and even for a particular day.

The following information is essential for forecasting:

- house count
- groups staying in hotel
- number of guests/groups staying on plans other than European plan
- parties
- conferences booked for the day and for the next few days.

The volume forecasting can be divided into two stages:

• *Initial Forecast*

Initial forecasting is a technique of predicting the volume of sale of the restaurant for a specific future period. It contains the number of meals to be served in each restaurant/outlet along with the type of items to be served. To have a nearly correct initial forecast the following information is collected:

a) **Sales History:** The sales of the same period during previous year and the preceding week's sale are examined for forecasting the next week's sales.

b) **Table Reservations:** Table reservations for all restaurants along with the menu and number of guests should be considered for making forecasts.

c) **Banquets, conferences:** All parties including banquets, conferences, kitty parties, etc. along with the expected number of guests and menu should be kept in mind while forecasting.

d) **Current Events**: Any happenings in the town like trade fairs, exhibitions being held nearby, will have a positive impact on the expected sale. On the contrary during marriage seasons, the walk in customers for meals and snacks reduce.

e) **Current Trends:** The current trends of selling or ordering menus should be considered. This can be picked up from the restaurant sales summary sheet/restaurant checks or from the kitchen summary sheet. The corrective measures wherever required should be taken to pick up the sale.

• ***Final Forecast***

The final forecasting is the predicting the volume of sales just a day before the preparation of the service of the particular meal. This forecasting is made after the initial forecast:

a) **Quantity of raw material:** After the dish wise sale, the quantity of basic raw material required to prepare those dishes is made. This is done in order to make right requisitions from stores and for placing orders/supply orders from purchase department to suppliers on time for the right quantity. This helps in reducing wastage and also avoids the chances of cancellation of orders due to non availability of raw materials.

b) **Quantity Order:** Purchase officer will evaluate the next week's requirements for the restaurants and will place the order with supplier keeping in mind the availability of store space, working capital, and management policy.

c) **Current day's requirement:** After checking the closing stock of raw material with the kitchens and stores, the purchase officer will place the order for the current day's perishable supply. He will also keep in mind the forecast for the day.

d) **Weather Condition:** In case the weather is not very conductive for people to go out will affect adversely on the restaurant sales through walk-ins. This will help purchase officer in finalizing the actual quantity of raw materials required for the day

FIXING OF STANDARDS

The word 'standard' is synonymous with phrase 'what it should be'. There are four different standards very essential for production control:

- Standard portion sizes
- Standard recipe
- Standard portion cost

Approval for these standards is obtained from the management. Consequently, only the management can approve any changes in the established standards. This means that although standards should not become so sacred that they never change, by the same token the changes that are made should reflect improved results once they are implemented and adopted by everyone in the organization. When a change is made, a new or revised standard exists and must be adhered to as was the previous standard.

STANDARD PORTION SIZES

A standard portion size represents the amount (weight, count, size or value)of each food item which is sold to the quest for a stated price and should be established for all items, including appetizers, main courses vegetables, salads, desserts and beverages.

ABC HOTELS LTD.

STANDARD PORTION SIZES 19...

ITEMS	PORTION SIZE	STATE OF PREPERATION RTE/RTC	OTHER DATA Ref. purchase specification or standard recipe

It is very important for hotels to have a standard portion size along with the standard recipe. If the size of the dish varies it can have an adverse effect on the marketing of menus. Even the restaurant staff will be confused as they themselves will not be very certain about the portion size.

If the standard portion size is not maintained then it will also affect on the maintenance of food cost.

Portion size charts written in large legible font must be displayed in each working area(butchery, bakery, etc). in addition each station must have portion scope, scales, measures and other equipment for standard portioning.

STANDARD RECIPES

A standard recipe is written formula for producing a food item of specified quality and quantity. **the standard recipe shows the exact quantity of each ingredient, the cost of making the item, and the sequence of steps to be followed in preparation.** To develop the best standard recipe the actual item must be prepared.

This requires full cooperation between the Food and Beverage Manager, Chef, F&B Controller, a progressive chef will work with management in preparing recipes covering his own food portions.

Objectives of preparing standard recipes:

1. **Quality and quantity of food ingredients:** the standard recipe helps in deciding the quantity and quality of raw material to be used for preparing a standard dish. It helps in making the *standard purchase specification* for each raw material for different dishes. E.g. the standard specification for tomatoes for green salad will be different from that of soup.
2. **Yield:** it helps in deciding the size of carcass or type of meat to be purchased to minimize the wastage. Standard recipes guide chef in fixing the size and weight of each portion and hence maximum yield can be generated from the raw material purchased.
3. **Food cost per dish:** it helps in maintaining the food cost of each and every dish and hence in maintaining gross profit.

Sale per dish –food cost per dish= GROSS PROFIT

4. **Nutritional value of the dish:** it is very useful especially for hostels, hospital, industrial canteens, cafeterias etc. The nutritional value can be accurate when known quantity and quality of raw material will be used.
5. **Menu planning:** it helps in planning menu as far as color, method of

cooking, basic raw material, etc. are concerned because the quantity and quantity of raw materials is known in advance.

ABC HOTELS Ltd.

UNIT RECIPE FOR .... No. OF PORTION:..................

PORTION SIZE:.....................

YIELD

Sr.	INGREDIENTS	QUANTITY	UNIT	%age LOSS	RATE			COST OF RAW MATERAIL	
					USABLE WEIGHT	IN SEASON	OFF SEASON	IN SEASON	OFF SEASON

COSTED FOR PROJECTIONS AND IMPRESSIONS: COST PRICE PORTION:

PREPERATION AND SERVICE:....................... TOTAL COST:

METHOD:PROCEDURE.............. SALE PRICE PER PORTION :

TIME.......... COST %age:

TEMPERATURE..................

Specimen recipe format

6. **Purchasing, requisitions and departmental transfers:** if the exact quantity and quality of each ingredient is known in advance because of correct forecasting and standard recipes then it helps in purchasing the raw material.

STANDARD PORTION COST

It is the cost of preparing and serving one portion of food or one drink according to the standard recipe.

It determined by dividing the cost of ingredients by the no. of portions.

Standard portion cost = total cost of ingredients No. of portions

PORTION COSTING SHEET

This sheet is very useful for medium and small size hotels which have no standard recipes. It helps to check the portion size of a dish. It also assists in costing of each dish in bulk or by portions.

$$\text{Standard portion cost} = \frac{\text{total cost of ingredients}}{\text{No. of portions}}$$

In this sheet food items are classified, and hence assists in purchasing of raw material.

COMPUTATION OF STAFF MEALS

Recording and analyzing of employee meals is important for production control. Controlling production cost in regards of employee meal is essential for control of cost. Factor like amount of employees, consumption of food, type of food, cost of meal, check on consumption etc should be always kept in mind. The following points are considered while computation of staff meal:

- **Separate requisition:** All the food used for the preparation of employee meals is issued separately through requisition. All such requisitions are kept separately and cost in order to determine the cost of employee meal.
- **Pre- establishment cost:** The management decides cost per meal and directs the chef that the cost of meal shouldn't be exceeding the pre-establishment cost. This amount is credited to food cost per employee. A record is kept of the employees who are feed each day. This record is multiplied to pre-establishment cost per meal which gives the cost of employee meals per day.
- **Elimination of cost of employee meal:** Specified number of Rs.1 day is credited to food cost to cover the cost of all employee meals regardless of the number of employee who actually eat. The chef will estimate the number who are expected to eat and will prepare the food. The cost of food so prepared should not exceed the cost guidelines.
- **Employees/staff check method:** All employees who eat are supposed to record their selection on the checks which are similar to guest check, prices are recorded next to cash selected item. The total is multiplied by average food cost percent in recent period to calculate the cost figure per employee meal for that period.

BACKGROUND INFORMATION

Several calculations are used in the industry to measure meal productivity:

- **Meals per labor hour**- this is calculated by dividing the total meals served by the total number of labor hours.

$$\frac{\textbf{Total meals served}}{\textbf{Total number of labor hours}}$$

- **Minutes per meal**- this is calculated by dividing the total labor hours X 60 minutes by the total number of meals.

$$\frac{\textbf{Total labor hours X 60}}{\textbf{total meals served}}$$

- **Labor hours per meal**- this is calculated by dividing the total hours per meal by the total meals served.

$$\frac{\textbf{Total labor hours}}{\textbf{Total meals served}}$$

QUESTIONNAIRE

1. What do you understand by the words "production control"? What are its aims and objectives?
2. How would you ensure production control? Discuss various production control method
3. Write short notes on the following:
   - Volume forecasting
   - Standard recipe
   - Standard portion size
4. What is forecasting? What are the various methods used for forecasting?
5. Explain about the objectives of volume forecasting.
6. What do you understand by standard fixing?
7. Write a short note on portion costing sheet.
8. Explain the different objectives of preparing standard recipe?
9. Write a big note on "COMPUTATION OF STAFF MEALS".

UNIT 6

SALES CONTROL

INTRODUCTION

Every Hotel needs proper and effective control system in order to run its operations smoothly and effectively, without any fraudulent activities.

This control is required at each and every stage of the Food and Beverage Cycle, i.e.:

1. Taking the customer's food or beverage order
2. Announcing these orders to kitchen or bar as the case may be
3. Getting the order correct and ready on time
4. Serving the correct order, on time with correct serving temperature to the guest
5. Making the correct bill
6. Setting the bill
7. Closing of the restaurant

Food sale is such a business if allowed unchecked can make an establishment bankrupt overnight. Therefore, it is not the workers or masters should work to control but system should work efficiently to prevent a disaster.

FUNCTIONS OF A CONTROL SYSTEM

- The control system monitors the area where food and beverage sales take place.
- It reduces the pilferage, fraud, and wastage to minimum.
- It provides required information to the management for costing purposes, so that they forecast the statistics accurately for the next financial period.
- It ensures that cashiers make bills correctly so that the customer is neither overcharged nor under charged.

- The food and beverage order taken from the guests should be documented for effective control. There are different checking methods followed for either of the two menu styles namely:
  i. Triplicate checking methods
  ii. Duplicate checking methods
  iii. Single order sheet
  iv. Quick service menu and customer bill "OR" Service with order
  v. Computerized order taking

TRIPLICATE K.O.T. CONTROL METHOD

This system is traditional and time tested and very efficient and still is vogue. As the name implies, the food check has 3 copies. Each copy has same serial number on them, and be off different color for easy identification and demarcation. Once the order is recorded on the KOT, the first copy goes to the kitchen or the dispense bar on the basis of which the order is prepared. Once the waiter picks up the order, the KOT copy is dropped in to the control box, which is always kept locked. Control box is maintained by the food and beverage control department to prevent any kind of fraud and malpractice.

TRIPLICATE K.O.T. CONTROL METHOD

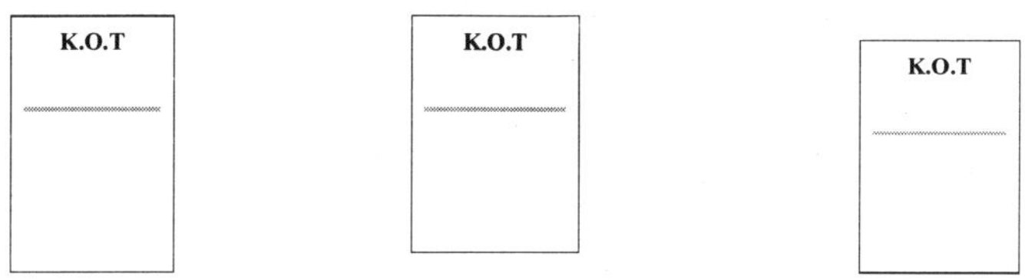

I- COPY	II- COPY	III-COPY
Sent to kitchen to collect the food against it.	Sent to the cashier to prepare the check.	retained in the book for the steward's record.

The second copy is given to the cashier, and based on that the bill is prepared, which has 2 copies. The first copy of the bill goes to guest and another copy is retained by the cashier the cashier attached the 2nd copy of KOT to the 2nd copy of the bill and submits it along with sales summary to the food and beverage controls at the end of the day.

The 3rd copy of KOT remains with the waiter in the KOT book for reference and checking up the order during service. It may be called for auditing at any time b the control department.

DUPLICATE CHECKING METHOD

This kind of checking method is used in small hotels, Cafés, and popular restaurants. As the name implies the KOT book has 2 copies. The first copy is sent to the kitchen on the basis of which the order is prepared. When the waiter picks up the order, the first copy is dropped in to the control box for auditing by the control department.

The waiter retains the second copy as a means of reference during the service. When guest requests for the billing, the waiter or cashier sum up all the rates on the 2nd copy of KOT and presents the same to the guest as the bill.

In a few organizations, the copy has four to five perforated slips. The waiter writes down the food order course wise on different perforated slips. As and when each course is required that particular slip is torn off and given at the hot plate. Every slip has a waiter number, table number, serial number and date. When the food is ready, the Aboyer keeps the particular slip along with the food to avoid confusion.

KITCHEN ORDER TICKET

MASALA ART
Multi Cuisine Restaurant

Date | Table No. | K.O.T. No.
Room No. | No. of pax. | Time

S. No.	Items	Qty

Waiter's Name Sign.................

KOT is prepared by food service personnel to intimate the food order of the guest to the kitchen staff. It helps in serving the right order to the right person. The KOT consists of details such as table number, covers, name of the waiter, date, time, items ordered, and its quantity. Usually, all the KOTs are serially numbered for control purpose. The food check may be duplicate or triplicate depending on the size and style of the organization.

A KOT is written as follows:

- The order is written along the lines and not up or down.
- Indication is given between the courses.
- If a few lines are left in KOT, that space is struck off.
- Quantity of each dish is written in words rather than the numbers....

SINGLE ORDER SHEET

This system is used in cafés, quick turn over restaurants, departmental stores, and taken away establishments; usually the menu is very limited with little or no choice. Many organizations following this system may have order sheet printed with the menu, after taking the order from the guests, the waiter writes it on KOT and calls for the order verbally over the hot plate. When the guest requests for the bill the waiter prices the order sheet and hand over to them as a bill. While leaving the restaurants, the guest submits the bill to the cashier and pays the amount. The cashier retains the bill for control purpose.

SERVICE WITH ORDER

This system of ordering is used in fast food joints, taken away, cafeterias, etc. Here the menu offered in the establishment is displayed in wall mounted boards. The guests choose what they want to eat and then order that. The person at the cash counter make the bill collects the cash, stamp the "bill received" and hand it over to the guest. The guest goes to respective food counter and collects the dishes against the bill. After delivering the order the person at the food counter stamps the bill "delivered" and hand it over to the guest.

Whatever may be the checking system used, it should ensure good control over the food service operation staff who deals with two important things—FOOD and CASH..

MODES OF PAYMENTS

There are various methods of making payments for the consumed food and beverage services. Some of the most popular methods are;

CASH

The payment received in cash should always be checked in front of the guest and at the same time when change is given then it should be counted back to customer. In this method complete payment is made in cash and therefore the currency notes should be checked for their authenticity and proper shape.

CREDIT CARDS

If the payment is made by credit **card**, the first step is to check its validity. Then a voucher is made out and filled in with the required details. The customer is then requested to sign the voucher after which the operator should check and match the signature with that on the credit card. The customer copy should be given to the guest.

The validity of the credit card is checked by passing it through the electronic machine after which the details of the credit card are printed on the form of itemized bill which the customer then signs. (One copy of this itemized bill is given to the customer for his record)

DEBIT CARDS

The use is similar to the above, but the amount used is immediately deducted from the customer's account.

CHEQUES

When accepted cheques, the cashier should check the following information;

- Correct date
- Filled amount (correct/incorrect)
- Signed by the person indicates on the cheque
- Match the signature of cheque card.

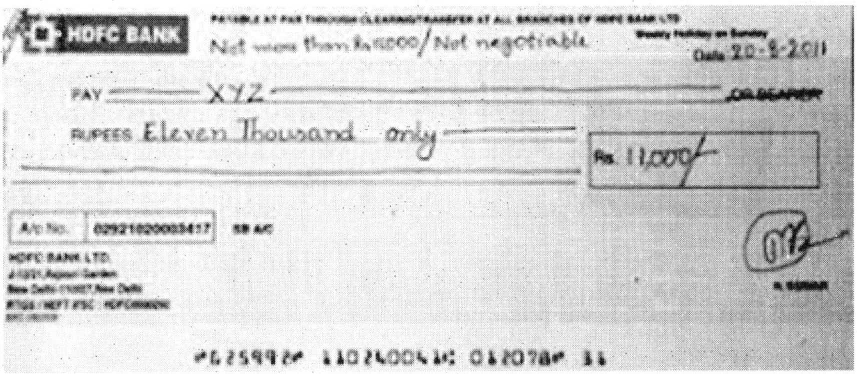

TRAVELLER'S CHEQUE

These may be issued by the travel agent (if travel agencies and hotels have tie up or any type of contract). The traveler's cheque must be signed once when issued and again when to pay.

SALES

A **sale** is the act of selling a product or service in return for money or other compensation. Signaling completion of the prospective stage, it is the beginning of an engagement between customer and vendor or the extension of that engagement.

The **seller** or **salesperson** – the provider of the goods or services – completes a sale in response to an acquisition or to an appropriation or to a request. There follows the passing of title (property or ownership) in the item, and the application and due settlement of a price, the obligation for which arises due to the seller's requirement to pass ownership. Ideally, a seller agrees upon a price at which he willingly parts with ownership of or any claim upon the item.

The purchaser, though a party to the sale does not execute the sale, only the seller does that. To be precise the sale completes prior to the payment and gives rise to the obligation of payment. If the seller completes the first two above stages (consent and passing ownership) of the sale prior to settlement of the price, the sale remains valid and gives rise to an obligation to pay.

INSIDE SALES VS. OUTSIDE SALES

Since the advent of the telephone, a distinction has been made between "inside sales" and "outside sales" although it is generally agreed that those terms have no hard-and-fast definition.

In the United States, the Fair Labor Standards Act defines outside sales representatives as "employees who sell their employer's products, services, or facilities to customers away from their employer's place of business, in general, either at the customer's place of business or by selling door-to-door at the customer's home" while defining those who work "from the employer's location" as inside sales.

Inside sales generally involves attempting to close business primarily over the phone, while outside sales will usually involve initial phone work to book sales calls at the potential buyer's location to attempt to close the deal in person. Some companies have an inside sales department that works with outside representatives and book their appointments for them. Inside sales sometimes refers to upselling to existing customers.

WAYS OF EXPRESSING SELLING

UPSELLING

Upselling is a good way to sell products to customers who are currently purchasing. With this method, no extra work, like finding a customer or cold calling, is necessary. Customers calling into your ordering department or visiting your store are your targets. For example, a customer wants to purchase XY product for $29. The salesperson informs the customer that the XYZ product for $39 has more features and a longer warranty. Upselling is easy because it combines selling products with good customer service.

DIRECT SALES

Direct-sales marketing can be expensive but effective. Sell your services or products through commercials on the Internet or local television channels. When customers see products they want to purchase, they call the contact number or visit the web store to make their immediate purchase.

UPGRADING

Offering clients upgrades is a good way to improve sales and improve customer care. Make a courtesy call to current clients to inform them of upgrades. As a reward for their customer loyalty, offer them a discount for making an immediate purchase.

BUNDLE SELLING

Selling one product at a time can make reaching sales goals time-consuming, even impossible. Instead of giving clients one product, bundle products. For example, pitch the entire skin care set rather than just a cleanser or moisturizer. You can always step down the sale if clients don't want a bundle.

INTERNET SALES

Internet sales through a reliable, secure website provides greater sales. Also, clients like web shopping because it is convenient and they don't have to battle crowds of people. Create an online catalog of the company's products with good descriptions, including prices, for each one. Some companies offer a discount for Internet customers; don't forget to budget for shipping.

CATALOG SALES

Many people like buying from catalogs. You should send customers a printed catalog featuring limited edition and regular products. Arrange the products by department or place seasonal products at the front of the catalog to capture holiday shoppers.

FAIRS AND EXPOS

If you like meeting people and holding demonstrations, fairs and expos are the perfect sales venue for you. You'll need to plan and pay for your product space. Spend some time making an inviting product display and be available to answer questions. Fairs and shows are often seasonal, so sales in this area my be limited.

STORE DISPLAYS

Small businesses that have store space should use store displays to generate sales. Many manufacturers offer sales kits that feature posters, stands and colorful banners. Arrange attractive shelving at eye level to make put your products in the customer's line of sight. Keep a well-stocked, tidy store for your customers to shop and buy.

HOME PARTIES

Selling via home party is a method many small-business owners use. Business owners book home parties as venues for showing products, giving samples and taking orders. Home parties create networks of customers who buy products in a casual, relaxed atmosphere. Some franchises don't allow franchisees to sell products in stores or fairs, making this method almost necessary for success.

EVENTS

Annual, quarterly and monthly events will maintain an excitement level at your business that will encourage customers to buy. Build sales activity by holding special events like grand openings, sales events, charity days and holiday shows. In-store fashion shows, focus groups and sample days are also good ways to sell products.

DETERMINING SALES PRICE

DETERMINE YOUR SELLING PRICE

Important terms

- Purchase price: this is the cost price – the price you pay to buy the product

- Mark-up: this is the amount you add to the purchase price to get the selling price
- Selling price: this is the retail price – the amount you sell the goods for.

Selling price = Purchase price + Mark-up

Mark-up is normally expressed as a percentage of the buying price.

What is 'sales'?

The term 'sales' is often used to mean the money you earn from the sale of your product or service. Sales may include:

- Money from products you have purchased and then sold
- Money you have earned from selling your labour and/or services
- Money you have earned by selling things you have made or assembled.

COST OF GOODS SOLD

After your business's first trading period, you'll need to calculate your profit. The first step in this process is determining the cost of goods sold.

One of the methods used to determine cost of goods sold is:

Cost of goods sold = Opening stock + Purchases – Closing stock

- Opening stock: is the stock you have in your business at the start of the trading period.
- Closing stock: is the stock you have in your business at the end of the trading period.

You should consider a number of issues in this calculation, such as the freight in, which refers to the cost of freight on the goods purchased. Seek professional advice when you calculate your cost of goods sold.

TOTAL SALES

It's important to understand the difference between mark-up and gross profit margin.

- Mark-up is the amount added to the buying price to determine the selling price.
- Gross profit margin is the percentage that gross profit is of the sales. It tells you what percentage of your sales is available to cover your expenses and give you a profit.

OPERATING EXPENSES

Operating expenses are expenses that a business incurs in its day-to-day operation.

Some examples of operating expenses include:

- Accounting fees
- Advertising
- Power
- Rent
- Vehicle expenses
- Wages
- Insurance
- Telephone
- Maintenance.

NET PROFIT

Now you can calculate your business's net profit by subtracting operating expenses from your gross profit. This is calculated in a profit and loss account. The profit and loss account is a financial report showing the gross profit, from the trading account, less the operating expenses to produce a net profit for the period.

CALCULATION OF SELLING PRICE

1. YOUR COSTS

If your rate doesn't include enough just to break-even, you're heading for trouble. The best thing to do is sum up all your costs and divide by the number of hours you think you can bill a year.

2. YOUR PROFIT

Somewhat related to your costs, you should always consider how much money you are trying to make above breaking even. This is business after all.

3. MARKET DEMAND

If what you do is in high demand, then you should be aiming to make your services more expensive. Conversely if there's hardly any work around, you'll need to cheapen up if you hope to compete.

4. INDUSTRY STANDARDS

It's hard to know what others are charging, but try asking around. Find out what larger businesses charge as well as other freelancers. The more you know about what others are charging and what services they provide for the money, the better you'll know how you fit in to the market.

5. SKILL LEVEL

Not every freelancer delivers the same goods and one would expect to pay accordingly. When I was a freelancing newbie I charged a rate of $25 an hour for my design, when I stopped freelancing recently my rate was $125 an hour. Same person, but at different times I had a different skill level and hence was producing a different result. Whatever your rate, expect it to be commensurate with your skill.

6. EXPERIENCE

Although often bundled with skill, experience is a different factor altogether. You may have two very talented photographers, but one with more experience might have better client skills, be able to foresee problems (and thus save the client time and money), intuitively know what's going to work for a certain audience and so on. Experience should affect how much you charge.

7. YOUR BUSINESS STRATEGY

Your strategy or your angle will make a huge difference to how you price yourself. Think about the difference between Revlon and Chanel, the two could make the same perfume but you would never expect to pay the same for both. Figure out how you are pitching yourself and use that to help determine if you are cheap'n'cheerful, high end or somewhere in between.

8. YOUR SERVICE

What you provide for your clients will also make a big difference to your price tag. For example you might be a freelancer who will do whatever it takes to get a job just right, or perhaps you are on call 24-7, or perhaps you provide the minimum amount of communication to cut costs. Whatever the case, adjusting your pricing to the type and level of service you provide is a must.

9. WHO IS YOUR CLIENT

Your price will often vary for different clients. This happens for a few reasons. Some clients require more effort, some are riskier, some are repeat clients, some have jobs you are dying to do, some you wouldn't want to go near with a stick. You should vary your price to account for these sorts of factors.

MATCHING COST WITH SALES

- In accrual accounting, the matching principle states that expenses should be recorded during the period in which they are incurred, regardless of when the transfer of cash occurs.

- Conversely, cash basis accounting calls for the recognition of an expense when the cash is paid, regardless of when the expense was actually incurred.
- If no cause-and-effect relationship exists (*e.g.,* a sale is impossible), costs are recognized as expenses in the accounting period they expired: *i.e.,* when have been used up or consumed (*e.g.,* of spoiled, dated, or substandard goods, or not demanded services). Prepaid expenses are not recognized as expenses, but as assets until one of the qualifying conditions is met resulting in a recognition as expenses.
- Prepaid expenses, such as employee wages or subcontractor fees paid out or promised, are not recognized as expenses; they are considered assets because they will provide probable future benefits.
- The matching principle allows for a more objective analysis of profitability. By recognizing costs in the period they are incurred, a business can see how much money was spent to generate revenue, reducing "noise" from timing mismatch between when costs are incurred and when revenue is realized.
- Expense vs. cash timing
    - Accrued expenses
    - Deferred expenses
    - Depreciation
- Two types of balancing accounts exist to avoid fictitious profits and losses that might otherwise occur when cash is paid out not in the same accounting periods as expenses are recognized, because expenses are recognized when obligations are incurred regardless when cash is paid out according to the matching principle in accrual accounting. Cash can be paid out in an earlier or latter period than obligations are incurred (when goods or services are received) and related expenses are recognized that results in the following two types of accounts:
    - Accrued expense: Expense is recognized before cash is paid out.
    - Deferred expense: Expense is recognized after cash is paid out.

ACCRUED EXPENSES

Is a liability with an uncertain timing or amount, but where the uncertainty is not significant enough to qualify it as a provision. An example is an obligation to pay for goods or services received from a counterpart, while cash for them is to be paid out in a later accounting period when its amount is deducted from accrued expenses.

DEFERRED EXPENSES

Is an asset, such as cash paid out to a counterpart for goods or services to be received in a latter accounting period when fulfilling the promise to pay is actually acknowledged, the related expense item is recognized, and the same amount is deducted from prepayments.

It shares characteristics with accrued revenue with the difference that an asset to be covered latter are proceeds from a delivery of goods or services, at which such income item is earned and the related revenue item is recognized, while cash for them is to be received in a later period, when its amount is deducted from accrued revenues.

EXAMPLES

- Accrued expense allows one to match future costs of products with the proceeds from their sales prior to paying out such costs.
- Deferred expense (prepaid expense) allows one to match costs of products paid out and not received yet.
- Depreciation matches the cost of purchasing fixed assets with revenues generated by them by spreading such costs over their expected life.

ACCRUED EXPENSES

For example, supplying goods in one accounting period by a vendor, but paying for them in a later period results in an *accrued expense* that prevents a fictitious increase in the receiving company's value equal to the increase in its inventory by the cost of the goods received, but unpaid. Without such accrued expense, a sale of such goods in the period they were supplied would cause that the unpaid inventory would effectively offset the sale proceeds resulting in a fictitious profit in the period of sale, and in a fictitious loss in the latter period of payment, both equal to the cost of goods sold.

DEFERRED EXPENSES

A Deferred expense is an asset used to costs paid out and not recognized as expenses according to the matching principle.

For example, when the accounting periods are monthly, an 11/12 portion of an annually paid insurance cost is added to prepaid expense, which are decreased by 1/12 of the cost in each subsequent period when the same fraction is recognized as an expense, rather than all in the month in which such cost is billed. The not-yet-recognized portion of such costs remains as prepayments (assets) to prevent such cost from turning into a fictitious loss in the monthly period it is billed, and into a fictitious profit in any other monthly period.

DEPRECIATION

Depreciation is used to distribute the cost of the asset over its expected life span according to the matching principle. If a machine is bought for $100, 000, has a life span of 10 years, and can produce the same amount of goods each year, then $10, 000 of the cost of the machine is matched to each year, rather than charging $100, 000 in the first year and nothing in the next 9 years. So, the cost of the machine is offset against the sales in that year. This matches costs to sales.

BILLING PROCEDURE

Many types of billing methods are used in foods service operations. The type of method used depends on style and volume of business. They are explained as follows;

BILL AS CHECK

In a duplicate checking system, the second copy of the food check is used as a bill. When the guest requests for the bill, the waiter or cashier sums up all the rates on the second copy of the KOT and presents the same to the guest. This method is used in small hotels, café, and popular restaurants.

SEPARATE BILLS

The bill is made for the second copy of the food check. The second is given to the cashier. Based on that, the cashier prepares a bill that has two copies. The top copy of the bill is presented to the guest. On receiving payment to the guest, the bill is stamped 'paid' and is returned to the guest. The second copy is retained to the cashier and attached to the second copy of KOT to submit it along with sale summery to the food and beverage controls department.

PRE-PAID

The customer purchases tickets or coupons in advance, either for specific meal or specific value. For example food service operations organizing theme food festivals, fashion shows, and New Year's Eve program sell admission tickets in advance at fixed price. Admission in to the venue and service of food and beverages is based on tickets or coupons.

NO-CHARGE

In this system, the guest is not charged for receiving the goods or services. The guest is asked only to sign the bill as acceptance of service received, and the particular amount is posted to the house.

DEFERRED

This type of system is used in catering function. In this, a service has been requested by an individual, firm, or company, which has been confirmed and taken place. Upon the conclusion of event, the bill is prepared or the services rendered and are sent to the company or organization person.

In the restaurants, when the guest request for the bill, the waiter collects it from the cashier and checks it whether all items are entered and priced correctly. It is always advisable for the waiter to double check the addition. Then the bill is presented to the guest in a bill folder.

BILL FORMAT

BILL

HOTEL XYZ
Diplomatic Enclave
New Delhi

Date	Reference no.

Vendor

Bill due
Terms
Memo

ITEMS

Item	Description	Qty	u/m	Cost	Amount	Customer. job	Class

COMPUTERIZED CHECKING SYSTEMS OR CONTROLLING SYSTEM

In today's food service operations, computer has become an integral part and is used in every sphere of operations. Computerized pre-check systems are extensively used in food and beverage control.

The advantages of using modern technology in food service operations are as follows;

- It ensures good control over the operations.
- It increases productivity and reduce labor costs.
- It eliminates revenue leakages by ensuring that all the orders are billed.
- It reduces clerical errors to minimum.
- It avoids duplication of work.
- It saves time.
- It generates bills quickly without any mistake.

ELECTRONIC CASH REGISTER

An electronic cash register is a mechanical device used to calculating and recording sales transactions. It usually prints a receipt for the customer. It has an attached drawer for storing cash. The cash drawer can be opened after a sale, except when special keys, which only senior employees have. This reduces the risk of cash pilferage.

ADVANTAGES

- Print checks, including the printing of previously entered items.
- Provide an analysis of sales by waiter per hour shift period.
- Provide an analysis of sales made by type of product.
- Analysis of sales by method of payment (cash, cheque, credit card, etc...)
- Complete automatic tax calculations and cover service charges.

SALES SUMMARY SHEET

The sales summary sheet is an analysis of all the transactions/cash taken during the particular period of service. It is prepared to know the revenue generated through the sales of food, beverages, the modes of bill settlement-cash, cheque, credit card, amount charged to room accounts, tax amount, discounts given etc. the basic information required in a sales summary sheet includes the following:

- Date
- Bill number
- Table number
- Number of cover per table
- Bill amount
- Modes of payment-cash, credit card, cheque, posted to room.

FORMAT OF REVENUE CONTROL SHEET OR SALE SUMMARY SHEET

RESTAURANT SALES SUMMARY SHEET											
ABC RESTAURANT											
Date					**Cashier**				**Scroll No.**		
Shift & Time							**Voucher No.**				
Meal											
S. no	**Voucher No.**	**K.O.T.**	**Steward's Name**	**Amount**	**Sales tax**	**Luxury tax**	**Discount**	**Service charge**	**Amount**		**remarks**
									Cash	**credit**	

Cash received
No. of cash vouchers
No. of credit card vouchers

Signature of cashier.................................
Signature of front office cashier..................

POINT OF SALE TERMINAL

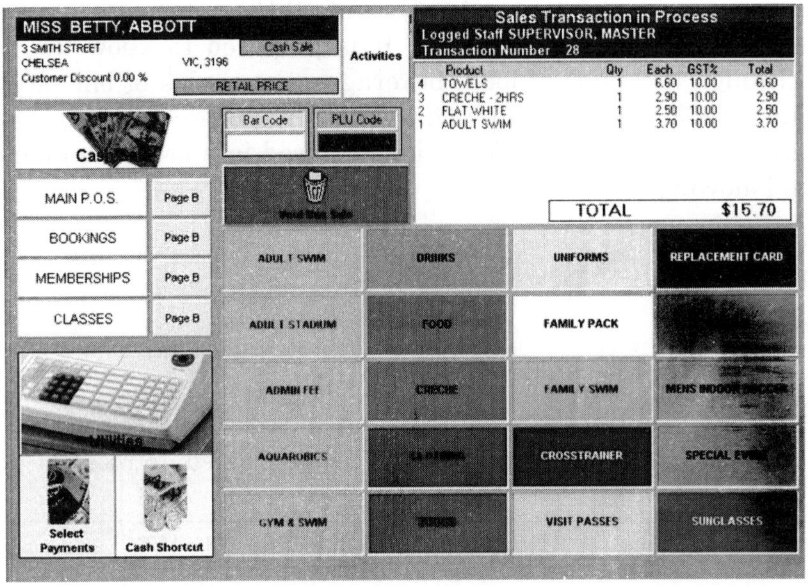

Point-of-sale systems are computerized system incorporating registers, computers and peripheral equipments, usually on a computer network. These systems keep track of sale & can generate records used in accounting and book keeping.

POS registers are connected to touch screen monitors, magnetic strip readers, bar code terminals, etc. the data is fed to various terminals and it can be accessed in various output units. This system integrates the data and reduces the manual work. For example- if a bill is made in the restaurant, it will be automatically posted in the guest bill, if a KOT is made it can be displayed in the kitchen or can be printed in the kitchen.

These systems can also generate reports required by various departments at any given point of time, can control reservations, guest history, guest registration, sale summary sheet etc.

QUESTIONNAIRE

1. Define Sales.
2. What is the formula of calculating COST OF GOOD SOLD?
3. What are the functions of a sales control system?
4. What is the difference between triplicate and duplicate method of KOT?
5. What are the ways of expressing selling?

6. What are the steps of calculating selling price?
7. What is billing procedure? Explain with the format?
8. What is an electronic cash register? What is it advantages?
9. Explain sales summary sheet with the help of a format?
10. What is POINT OF SALE (POS)?
11. What are the different types of expenses?

UNIT 7

COST DYNAMICS

COST

Cost is generally defined as reduction in the value of assets for the purpose of securing benefits or gains in the food beverage business, cost means the price to the hotel or restaurants of goods and services when the good are consumed or the services rendered.

COSTING

Costing may be defined as the technique and process of ascertaining costs. Costing means simply the process of arithmetic, means of memorandum statements or the methods of integral control.

The cost of any item may be expressed in a variety of ways such as:

Units of weight, unit of volume, total per individual portion

For example, the cost of liquor can be expressed in terms of the cost per bottle, per drink, or per ounce.

The following are the methods of costing:

1. **Batch costing:** The identification and assignment of costs related to producing a set amountt of goods. This includes all fixed and variable cost for producing the batch.
2. **Job costing:** It involves the calculation of costs involved in a construction "job" or the manufacturing of goods done in discrete batches.
3. **Contract costing:** Contract Costing is a special type of job costing where the unit of cost is a single contract. Contract itself is a cost centre and is executed under the customer's specifications.
4. **Operation costing and process costing:** Process costing is an accounting methodology that traces and accumulates direct costs and

allocates indirect costs of a manufacturing process. Costs are assigned to products, usually in a large batch, which might include an entire month's production.

5. **Unit, output and operating costing:** In finance, unit cost is the cost of a single no. product and output cost is the cost required to produce a good output and operating cost is the cost to carry on operations well.
6. **Marginal costing:** In finance, marginal cost is the change in the total cost that arises when the quantity produced has an increment by unit. That is, it is the cost of producing one more unit of a good. In general terms, marginal cost at each level of production includes any additional costs required to produce the next unit.
7. **Food and beverage sales:** Food & Beverage cost is an important activity in the hotel industry. It deals with the techniques to setup and maintain total cost control systems which can help have to earn profits in the business.

CONCEPT OF COSTING

1. To know cost
2. To fix the selling price
3. Cost controlling
4. Preparation of profit and loss account and balance sheet Operating policies of the organisation.

ADVANTAGES OF COSTING

1. Helps in proper planning of the food & beverage operations
2. Keeps a control check over the accuracy of financial accounts
3. Helps in the pricing of menu, dishes & beverages
4. Helps in comparing cost per unit of a specific period or two or more periods of time
5. Somewhat specifies how the hotel is into profit or loss
6. Helps in proper understanding of the quality and packaging of material or goods
7. Develops an effective costing system and controls the cost
8. Helps in making closing stock value sheet

ELEMENTS OF COST

1. Material Cost/Food cost
2. Labour Cost
3. Overhead cost

1. Material Cost: In material cost or food cost one has to take into account the opening stock, purchases and closing stock and the food consumed by staff or served as complimentary to guests usually spoilage of food is charged to the material cost.

TOTAL MATERIAL COST PERCENTAGE

= total material cost*100/total sale

To Control The Food Cost One Must Remember The Following Points:

a) **Purchasing** – The purchase department must ensure that the right quality of food is purchased at competitive price and right quantity of raw materials should be procured to keep a control over food cost.

b) **Receiving and storing of raw material** – the raw material received by stores must be inspected for the quantity, quality and specifications. All material received must be stored at proper place. No food item should get spoiled.

c) **Issuing** – All goods should be issued after a proper requisition, the store keeper must follow FIFO, LIFO according to their store policy.

d) **Wastage & Spoilage** – The wastage of portioning, storing, cooking should be as minimum as possible

e) **Proper Storing Of Cooked Food** – In case of the cooked food is left at end of day then it must be stored at proper temperature and at proper place.

f) **Ensure No Food Is Served Without bill** – Incase the food is allowed to be picked up without proper bill, then this will increase the food cost.

g) **Portion Control** – The chef must ensure that dish is served as per the standard portion. A large portion will increase the food cost and a small portion will dissatisfy the guest.

h) **Standard recipe** – The chef must ensure that always standard recipe should be followed or otherwise the guest may not find the similar standard of dish and this will dissatisfy him.

2. Labour Cost: Apart from wages and salaries, all other expenses incurred of staff or on its welfare like medical re-imbursement, leave travel concession(L.T.C.), contribution towards the Employee's Provident Fund(E.P.F.), free food, uniform, accommodation, interest subsidy on loan, telephone bills etc.

TOTAL LABOURS COST PERCENTAGE

= total labour cost*100/total sale

Points to be considered to control labour cost:

1. The hotel must retain some of his staff as the new staff will take some time in adjusting till then they will give less output.
2. Most of the hotels lose money due to over staffing as it increases labour cost.
3. Over staffing does not improve quality of service.
4. Hotels must reduce overheads and other expenses on staff like on accommodation, food, interest subsidy, L.T.C. etc.
5. If sale increases the labour cost percentage to sale will come down and vice versa
6. Hotel may close any particular cuisine in any outlet if the cuisine is not doing well, to reduce the labour cost.

3. Overhead Cost: All other costs like office expenses, rent, interest, light and power, commission, water, gas, fuel, cooking coke and wood. Advertisement and marketing expenses, miscellaneous expenses, etc. are included under this head.

TOTAL OVERHEAD COST PERCENTAGE

= total overhead cost *100/total sale

Points to be considered to control overhead cost:

1. The hotel must study each and every cost deeply and in detail.
2. Hotel can consult the consultants.
3. The most common overhead cost is interest.
4. The debt should not be increased as it can become burden.
5. The overhead cost should not affect the quality of goods/services as it can reduced.

CLASSIFICATION OF COST

COST CONCEPTS

It may be defined as classifying, recording, and appropriate allocation of expenditure for the determination of the cost of the products or services and the presentation of suitably arranged data for the purpose of control and guidance for the management.

The total cost of the product or service can be classified according to the transactions involved or the origin of the cost.

The types of the cost can be classified thus on two different basis–

(a) Type of Expenditure

(b) In view of behavior of cost

TYPE OF EXPENDITURE: On the type of Expenditure cost can be divided into: Direct costs and Indirect costs.

Direct cost: Direct cost can be divided further into –

1. **Direct Material cost:** This includes the cost of materials which enter into and become the part of food and beverage produced. Ex- flour.
2. **Direct Labor cost:** This includes all the wages paid to employee who are immediately concerned with the production. Ex-salary of chef.
3. **Direct Expenses:** this includes all expense which can be directly identified with the product. Ex-cost of special tools.

Indirect cost: This includes all the cost which cannot be identified with a particular product or service. The incurrence of such cost is on behalf of the business as a whole. These can be further classified as –

Production overheads: This includes the following –

- Wages paid to the repairmen.
- Workers welfare expense.
- Social securities.
- Buying and storekeeping expenses.
- Rent and rates.
- Insurance.
- Power and fuels.
- Depreciation

Office and administrative expenses: This includes the following

- Rent, insurance and lighting of office premise.
- Salaries paid to administrative staff.
- Stationeries, postage.
- Bank charges.
- Audit fees.
- Legal charges.

Selling and Administration expenses: This includes the following:

- Salaries of sales director.
- Traveling expenses and commission payable.
- Advertising expenses.
- Printing of catalogue.
- Bad debts.
- Subscriptions to hotel, tourism and travel agencies.

IN VIEW OF BEHAVIOR OF COSTS: On the basis of behavior of costs the costs can be divided into" fixed cost, variable cost and semi variable cost.

Fixed cost: The behavior of these costs is such that it remains un-effected by the change in the volume of business. This is certainly a major hindrance towards profitability. Examples of such cost are:

- Rent and rates.
- Repairs
- Interest
- Employees remuneration
- Maintenance

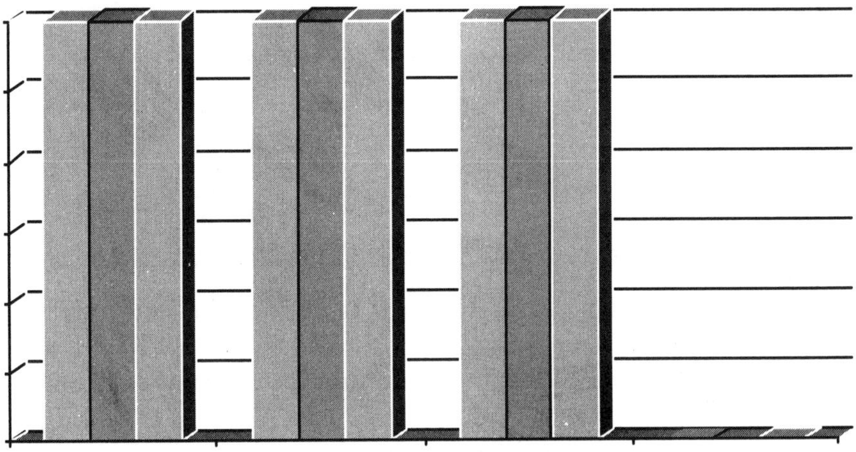

Variable cost: The behavior of the cost is such that it varies in the direct proportion to the changes in the volume of sale. Examples of such costs are

- Food cost
- Laundry cost
- Beverage cost

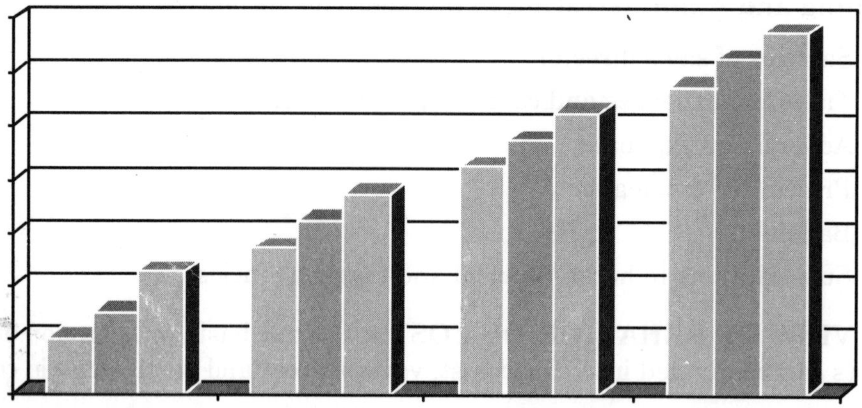

Semi-variable: The behavior of these costs is such that it varies with changes in volume of sales but not in direct proportion to changes. These costs remain constant over a relative short range of sales volume but changes to a new level with an increase or decrease in the volume of activity.eg. Telephone Charges.

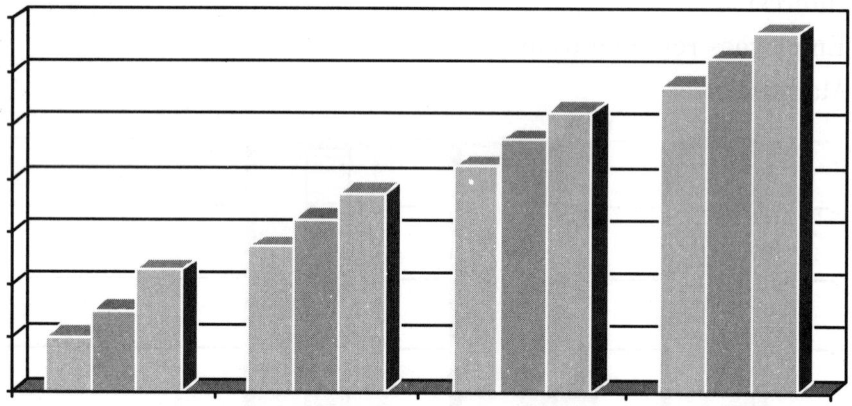

Marginal Costing: This is also known as variable costing. In this system the total variable cost of the unit of output is ascertained. It deals primarily with changes in future cost. It can be defined as the increase in total cost resulting from one more unit being produced. In calculation of Marginal costing certain number of units are considered instead of a single unit.

ADVANTAGES OF MARGINAL COSTING

- Breakeven point can be calculated.
- Profit planning.
- Decision making.

- Determination of selling price.
- Submitting tenders and quotation.
- Cost control & Sales mix

QUESTIONNAIRE

1. What is cost and costing?
2. Explain the methods of costing?
3. What are the advantages of costing?
4. Explain the Elements of cost?
5. Mention the points to be considered while controlling food cost, labour cost amd overhead cost?
6. What is classification of cost and explain cost concepts?
7. Briefly explain the fixed cost, variable cost and semi-variable cost with the help of graphic diagrams?
8. What are the advantages of marginal costing?

UNIT 8

SALES CONCEPT

DEFINITION

Sales is defined as revenue resulting from the exchange of products and services for value.

It can be defined as Restaurateur's exchange of product or service for the value. The value may cash or a promise to pay cash in some future time, as in case of credit card sales. Cost was defined as reduction in the assets. A sale is opposite to cost. Accountant defines the sales as an inflow of assets occurring as results of doing business.

There are two basic groups of terms normally used terms used in F&B operations to express sales concept. Ie. Monetary and non-monetary terms.

Monetary terms include:

1. total sales
2. total sales by category
3. total sales per server
4. Total sales per seat
5. Sales price
6. Average sale

Non-monetary terms include:

1. Total no. sold
2. Covers
3. Total covers
4. Average cover

5. Seat turnover
6. Sales mix

VARIOUS SALES CONCEPTS

RUPEE SALES

Sales is basically expressed in monetary terms for the value of goods or services and only basic cost is given. It normally does not include the taxes and tips, which if applicable must be added to the basic selling price. If the state govt. imposes the tax it must be added to the bill given to customers. In addition, a tip is not normally included in selling price.

UNIT SALES

It is basically expressed in terms of quantity of unit sold. For the purpose of control it is expressed in that fashion of concern. Even though there is no monetary value associated but he number will be important for control. If 100 steaks were prepared and 80 were delivered to kitchen and 20 were returned as unsold. So we can determine the total sale for steak by multiplying it with selling price.

AVERAGE RUPEE SALES

The management may be interested in the average sale that is the average check per customer, because it directly indicates how well the menu is working as well as the effectiveness of overall selling efforts. It also help to determine if the price are too high or low. The average check price is normally calculated for the meal each day. To determine it, the total value of all sales of day is divided by number of customers. The manager will watch the average check price over a period of time to determine if corrective action should be taken or if investigation into preparation, service or pricing should be made.

SALES PER WAITER

It may be expressed in mainly two different ways. One way is to express it as the number of customers served by per waiter. This figure will give some indication of efficiency of service personnel and provide a basis for better scheduling, training needs of individual waiter, motivation corrective action etc.

Another way of expressing sales per waiter is in terms of Rupee. The total sale is for a period of time per waiter is divided by the number of customer he serves. Management would able to single out better sales personnel.

SALES PER TIME PERIOD

Total Rupee sales and total number of sales per hour, day, week and month are important when it comes to scheduling personnel and opening and closing hours, as well as providing better services to customers. E.g A restaurant might havegrossed Rs. 50000/- for three hour lunch period and grossed only Rs, 5000/- for three hours thereafter. The number of personnel scheduled for the period would be considerable different.

If it has been established that one waiter can serve twenty customers per hour with optimal efficiency and high standards of service, the manager is interested in the total number of customer served per hour in the order that the standard of service can be better measured.

MAXIMISING SALES

Every manger is trying constantly to increase the sales in order that profit can be maintained or increased in the face of constant higher costs. In attempting to maintain profitability, one must recognize those factors that cause customers to patronize food operation over another. They are as follows

1. Location of Business
2. Differentiated Product
3. Acceptable Price
4. Pleasing Décor
5. Portion Sizes
6. Quality Product services
7. Variety of Menu Items

The factors are not ranked in any particular order. Every customer has his own important reason for patronizing a restaurant, and these will change under varying circumstances. To some, the food quality might be single important factors for patronizing one restaurant over any other and for some it might be location for other it might be prices of menu items etc.

MATCHING COST WITH SALES

In order for the Restaurateur to stay profitably in business total sales must be greater than total cost. If cost exceeds the sale for extended period of time, the owner will confront bankruptcy or he has to put additional funds business into order to keep it going. It is job of cost controller or manager to be constantly aware e of costs of operating the business and to keep them below sales. Costs of operation are gathered on daily basis and compared with daily sales and various types of cost to sales ratios are determined.

These ratios are compared. with previous year ration of same time period and judgment are made whether they satisfactory or not. If not the remedial action are taken to bring down cost to point where the ratios are satisfactory.

PRICING METHODS

It is very difficult to fix the price of the menu or dish.

The following are some pricing methods:

1. Food cost
2. Competitive Price
3. Reasonable Price
4. The Ratio Price Method
5. Trail and error Method
6. Highest Price Guest Can Pay
7. Aggressive selling
8. Mark a Price
9. No pricing

    1. **Food cost** – In india it is the most common method of fixing price, before fixing the price, the portion size and the food cost of the dish is calculated. After knowing the food cost the selling price is decided.
    2. **Competitive price** – This price is fixed according to the competition present in the hotels markets, shops, and restaurants.
    3. **Reasonable Price** – The management or the owner uses various perspectives policies regulation in fixing the pricing and rates of dishes. Reasonable prices should be fixed on the guest ability pay for the services rendered and prices should also reflect on profits and gains or income.
    4. **The ratio and price method** – the previous years food and cost and selling prices of the goods are analysed and calculated which are kept for the records and the books and management keeping thet as a banch mark decides the future, selling price and sales method for the business.
    5. **Trial And Error Method** – this type of method is followed by the management for fixing the pricing menu and in this a price is fixed for the services of the goods and if the management is not satisfied with the prices, they are not able to earn desired profits or income, then the price is suitably changed suitability till the most effective price is achieved.

6. **Highest Price Guest Can Pay** – the management estimates about the maximum price guest can pay for the services or good given and this includes the upselling and cross-selling method also.
7. **Aggressive Selling** – many of the dishes are priced aggressively very low to attract more no. of guest, the prices of the two dishes may be as low as cost price or lower than cost price. These are used to increase their sales.
8. **Mark a Price** – This method is applicable in case of products which are not prepared inside the hotel or restaurants and are purchased from the outside market. these products are traded inside the hotel or restaurants with extra charges eg. Cold aerated drinks, alcoholic drinks, cigaretes.
9. **No pricing** – If any dish is not in the menu, and hotel serves that dish on special request, the price is first told to the guest and after it is accepted the food dish is served.

QUESTIONNAIRE

1. What is sales?
2. How is sales differentiated in monetary and non-monetary terms?
3. What are the various sales concepts?
4. List the factors helpful in maximising the sales?
5. What are the different pricing methods used in sales enhancement?
6. What is error and trial method. How it is useful in setting prices?
7. Explain the different pricing methods used in an f&b outlet.

UNIT 9

INVENTORY CONTROL

DEFINITION

Inventory can be described as the stock of goods and raw material, including perisables and non-perisables items kept in stores for present and future uses.

Inventory control can be described as the technique of maintaing and checking the stock.

The stock control involves purchasing, requisitions, receiving, storing, issuing to various departments.

OBJECTIVES

- To ensure corrective supply of material and other finished goods, so that production should not suffer at anytime.
- To avoid both under stocking and over stocking.
- To maintain investments in working capital at the minimumlevel that is required according to the operations and sales.
- To keep operating cost under control.
- To minimize the loss through depreciation, pilferage, wastage or damage etc.
- To design a proper inventory management system for the hotel.
- To ensure perpetual inventory control so that stock shown in the stock level should be actually used and properly stored in the respective stores and places.
- To ensure right quantity and quality goods at a reasonable prices.
- To facilitate furnishing of gata for a short and long term planning

- To compare the usage of food with food sales to calculate the food percentage and gross profits.
- To dertimine the value of goods held in stock.
- To list slow moving items, this will bring to the attention of the purchasing officer, the head chef, etc. Those items that are in stock and for which there has been no demand, since the last stocktaking.

METHODS

- Physical inventory
- Perpetual inventory

PHYSICAL INVENTORY

- A periodic actual counting of all the products in the storage areas.
- Actual counting is recorded on the basis of checks which can be once a week or a fortnight, a month.
- Physical counting is done before normal opening time or closing time of store or after closing.
- In large organisation, inyventories are taken in parts on weekly basis.
- Inventory process involves atleast two persons- one from controls and other from accounts department.
- One person counts systematically arranged stock and other person records the data on a physical inventory form.
- This form helps in taking physical inventory in shortest possible time.

Physical Inventory Form						
S. No.	Quantity in hand	Unit size	Food item	description	Unit cost	Total cost
Taken by...............				C/F inventory..............		

PERPETUAL INVENTORY SYSTEM

- Perpetual maintaining a continous records of all purchases and issued items.
- It provides a continous record of goods available on hand at any point of time.
- It is used to restrict the product in the dry and cold or frozen stores.
- It requires a considerable amount of labour to maintain the proper system working.
- It usually used for maintaining selected or expensive items.
- It is necesary to be tallied to physical inventory total amounts at end.

Perpetual Inventory Form (for storeroom)				
Item............			**Store room............**	
Date	Order no.	Quantity in	Quantity out	Quantity in hand

Perpetual Inventory Form (for bar)						
Date	Item	Brought forward	Quantity in	Quantity out	Balance C\F	Remarks

TOOLS AND TECHNIQUES OF INVENTORY CONTROL

In all types of food service operations efficient inventory control is very important. The major function of control system is to coordinate activity influencing in decisions and actions to ensure that the objectives are being met by providing feedback on operations, ensuring adequate production and needed service while minimizing inventory investments.

To fulfil the above objectives, the control and management role has become more complicated and critical. Variety of tools is available to assist management in determining quantity of purchase and recommends stock levels to determining costs of maintaining stock.

The following are the techniquesused in the industry for controlling stocks:

- **ABC Analysis:** In most restaurant/hotel operations, a small no. Of purchased items a/c for the major portion of the inventory purchase value. Therefore, a method for classifying purchase items according to the value is often admissible. The procedures is generally reffered to as ABC Analysis.

The purchase items should be divided into 3 categories:

1. **'A' Class:** This category represents only 15-20% of the inventory items but typically a/c for 75-80% of the total value of inventory. Thses items should be renewed continuously to estimate requirements to check stock balance and to determine the quantity of material to order.
2. **'B' Class:** This category consist of lesser value items that typically vary between 20-25% of items inventory and 10-15% of the total inventory value.
3. **'C' Class:** This category comprises of items which constitutes 60-65% of items inventory and inventory value is very less.

MINI MAX METHOD

1. Most widely used method of controlling inventories.
2. It involves the establishment of minimum and maximum levels of inventory and hence reffered as minimax method.
3. A safety factor stock is established which becomes the minimum point, below which the inventory should not fall under normal circumstances.
4. The maximum inventory consist of the safety factors plus the correct ordering quantity.
5. The safety factor is the backup supply to ensure against certain rise in usual rate which results due to the failure to ordered material or clerical errors in inventory records.
6. The size of safety factordepends on the importance of items in the operations, the value of the investmentand the availability of substitute on short notice.

7. The safety factor stock can be determined by the following factors:
   - Lead time:
     - o It is the interval between the time of requisition is initiated and the product is received.
     - o The shortest lead time occurs when material is purchased from alocal supplier.
     - o The longest lead time occurs when the material are ordered from out of down supplier.
   - Usage rate:
     - o Particular period is determimed by past expeience, forecast and by the length of time required to obtain deliveries.
     - o Minimum order point is established from this data.
     - o The minimum order point is the lowest stock levelthat can be safety maintained to avoid emergency purchasing.
     - o The maximum inventory level is equal to estimated usage plus the safety stock.

LEVELS OF INVENTORY CONTROL

ECONOMIC ORDER QUANTITY - EOQ

Definition of 'Economic Order Quantity' (EOQ): An inventory-related equation that determines the optimum order quantity that a company should hold in its inventory given a set cost of production, demand rate and other variables. This is done to minimize variable inventory costs. The full equation is as follows:

$$EOQ = \sqrt{\frac{2SD}{PI}}$$

where :

S = Setup costs
D = Demand rate
P = Production cost
I = Interest rate (considered an opportunity cost, so the risk-free rate can be used)

RELATED DEFINITIONS

- **Inventory**

  The raw materials, work-in-process goods and completely finished goods that are considered to be the portion of a business's assets that are ready or will be ready for sale. Inventory...

- **Enterprise Resource Planning - ERP**

  A process by which a company (often a manufacturer) manages and integrates the important parts of its business. An ERP management information system integrates areas such as planning,...

- **Multinational Corporation - MNC**

  A corporation that has its facilities and other assets in at least one country other than its home country. Such companies have offices and/ or factories in different countries and...

Definition of 'Zero-Based Budgeting - ZBB':

- A method of budgeting in which all expenses must be justified for each new period. Zero-based budgeting starts from a "zero base" and every function within an organization is analyzed for its needs and costs. Budgets are then built around what is needed for the upcoming period, regardless of whether the budget is higher or lower than the previous one.

  ZBB allows top-level strategic goals to be implemented into the budgeting process by tying them to specific functional areas of the organization, where costs can be first grouped, then measured against previous results and current expectations.

- **'Zero-Based Budgeting - ZBB'**

  Because of its detail-oriented nature, zero-based budgeting may be a rolling process done over several years, with only a few functional areas reviewed at a time by managers or group leadership.

  Zero-based budgeting can lower costs by avoiding blanket increases or decreases to a prior period's budget. It is, however, a time-consuming process that takes much longer than traditional, cost-based budgeting. The practice also favors areas that achieve direct revenues or production; their contributions are more easily justified than in departments such as client service and research and development.

There are various steps involved in the preparation of the budget and they are listed here.The preparation of a budget for any organization is a very important phase of the company. Each year the budget is revised and also looked at. The reason for this is that the budget usually outlines a framework within which the company can work. It also gives a broad framework to identify if the company will have a profit or a loss and this in turn will help to reassess the goals of the company and do appropriate changes in it.

1. ESTIMATE LONG AND SHORT TERM NEEDS OF THE COMPANY

The various long term needs also should be part of the budget. The main reason for the formulation of the budget is due to the fact that the long term needs of the company should be identified and the budget should try to lead the company toward the goal. Other than that, the short term goals which are the planning for the immediate year should also be done at the time of the budget.

2. CALCULATE THE INCOME FOR THE PAST YEAR, PRESENT YEAR AND FOR THE ENSUING YEAR

The income of the company for the past and the present year should be compared. Various facts should be taken into consideration and the person or the company should be able to calculate the possible income for the next year too. This will again act as a guideline for the company to function to try and achieve the immediate goals.

3. JUSTIFY THE ESTIMATED INCOME AND EXPENDITURES

Budget is a time when the previous year's income and the expenditure are assessed and the justification for the income and also the expenditure is given, if there is a change in the income that was forecast and the actual income generated. This will help to have accountability and also for the people concerned to take the whole exercise of budget seriously.

4. ESTIMATE THE COSTS

The cost of various aspects is also to be estimated during the year. This will make it very easy for the company to tackle any problems during the course of the year. Usually estimations during budget time also leave a contingency fund that can be used to tackle any emergency need of funds.

5. SET BUDGET IN ACCORDANCE WITH THE PHILOSOPHY OF THE INSTITUTION

The philosophy of one institution varies from that of another institution. The philosophy could be the allocation of funds for a specific cause which is the primary goal of the organization. This should be kept in mind at the time of the preparation of the budget.

6. REQUEST FOR SUFFICIENT FUNDS

Another important step in the preparation of the budget is that the financial management of the company that makes the budget can also ask for a specific amount of money for them to tide over certain activities that need to be done. The request for the funds can be made to the authorities concerned.

These are the various important steps of preparing the budget.

DEFINITION OF 'MARGIN OF SAFETY'

- A principle of investing in which an investor only purchases securities when the market price is significantly below its intrinsic value. In other words, when market price is significantly below your estimation of the intrinsic value, the difference is the margin of safety. This difference allows an investment to be made with minimal downside risk.

  The term was popularized by Benjamin Graham (known as "the father of value investing") and his followers, most notably Warren Buffett. Margin of safety doesn't guarantee a successful investment, but it does provide room for error in an analyst's judgment. Determining a company's "true" worth (its intrinsic value) is highly subjective. Each investor has a different way of calculating intrinsic value which may or may not be correct. Plus, it's notoriously difficult to predict a company's earnings. Margin of safety provides a cushion against errors in calculation.

- **'Margin of Safety'**

  Margin of safety is a concept used in many areas of life, not just finance. For example, consider engineers building a bridge that must support 100 tons of traffic. Would the bridge be built to handle exactly 100 tons? Probably not. It would be much more prudent to build the bridge to handle, say, 130 tons, to ensure that the bridge will not collapse under a heavy load. The same can be done with securities. If you feel that a stock is worth $10, buying it at $7.50 will give you a margin of safety in case your analysis turns out to be incorrect and the stock is really only worth $9.There is no universal standard to determine how wide the "margin" in margin of safety should be. Each investor must come up with his or her own methodology.

WHAT IS BIN CARD?

Bin card is a record of receipt and issue of materials Quantity of store received is entered with receipt column and the quantity of store issued is recorded in the issue column of Bin Card. Balance of quantity of stores is ascertained after every receipt or issue. It shows the balance of the stock at any moment of time. Bin Card is maintained by the store-keeper. He is answerable for any difference between physical store and the balance shown by the Bin Card. Thus Bin Card does not only records the receipt an issue of the stores but also assist the store keeper for control of the stock. For each item of stores minimum level maximum level, and ordering level are shown in the part of the Bin Card. By seeing the Bin Card the store keeper sends the material requisition for the purchase of materials from time to time.

A bin card is also known as bin tag or stock card and is usually hung up or placed in shelf, rack or bin where the material has been kept. Bin cards can also be in the form of loose sheets which can be maintained in a ledger kept in the stores.

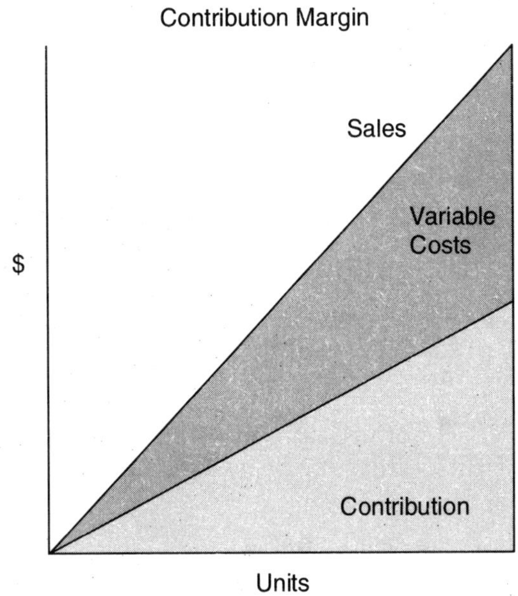

Decomposing Sales as Contribution plus **Variable Costs.** In the **Cost-Volume-Profit Analysis** model, costs are linear in volume.

In cost-volume-profit analysis, a form of management accounting, contribution margin is the marginal profit per unit sale. It is a useful quantity in carrying out various calculations, and can be used as a measure of operating leverage. Typically, high contribution margins are prevalent in the labour-intensive tertiary sector while low contribution margins are prevalent in the capital-intensive industrial sector.

DEFINITION

The Unit Contribution Margin (C) is Unit Revenue (Price, P) minus Unit Variable Cost (V):

$$C = P - V$$

The Contribution Margin Ratio is the percentage of Contribution over Total Revenue, which can be calculated from the unit contribution over unit price or total contribution over Total Revenue:

$$\frac{C}{P} = \frac{P-V}{P} = \frac{\text{Unit Contribution Margin}}{\text{Price}} = \frac{\text{Total Contribution Margin}}{\text{Total Revenue}}$$

For example, if the price is Rs10 and the unit variable cost is Rs2, then the unit contribution margin is Rs8, and the contribution margin ratio is Rs8/Rs10 = 80%.

Profit and Loss as Contribution minus Fixed Costs.

Contribution margin can be thought of as the fraction of sales that contributes to the offset of fixed costs. Alternatively, unit contribution margin is the amount each unit sale adds to profit: it's the slope of the Profit line.

Cost-Volume-Profit Analysis (CVP): assuming the linear CVP model, the computation of Profit and Loss (Net Income) reduces as follows:

$$\begin{aligned} PL &= TR - TC \\ &= (C + V) \times X - (TFC + V \times X) \\ &= C \times X - TFC \end{aligned}$$

where TC = TFC + TVC is Total Cost = Total Fixed Cost + Total Variable Cost and X is Number of Units. Thus Profit is Unit Contribution times Number of Units, minus the Total Fixed Costs.

The above formula is derived as follows:

From the perspective of the matching principle, one breaks down the revenue from a given sale into a part to cover the Unit Variable Cost, and a part to offset against the Total Fixed Costs. Breaking down Total Costs as:

$$TC = TFC + V \times X$$

one breaks down Total Revenue as:

$$\begin{aligned} TR &= P \times X \\ &= ((P - V) + V) \times X \\ &= (C + V) - X \\ &= C \times X + V \times X \end{aligned}$$

Thus the Total Variable Costs TVC = V × X offset, and the Net Income (Profit and Loss) is Total Contribution Margin minus Total Fixed Costs:

$$\begin{aligned} PL &= TR - TC \\ &= (C + V) \times X - (TFC + V \times X) \\ &= C \times X - TFC \\ &= TCM - TFC \end{aligned}$$

DIFFERENCES BETWEEN BUDGETARY CONTROL AND STANDARD COSTING

Although budgetary control and standard costing both are based on some common principles; both are pre-determined, comparison will be made with the actual costs and both system need a revision of the standards or the budget, these two systems have certain differences which are as follows:

1. Budgetary control deals with the operation of a department or the business as a whole in terms of revenue and expenditure. Standard costing is a system of costing which makes a comparison between standard costs of each product or service with its actual cost.
2. Budgetary control covers as a whole in terms of revenue and expenditures such as purchases, sales, production, finance etc. Standard costing is related to a product and its cost only.
3. Budgetary control is applicable to utmost all business organizations. Standard costing is applicable to manufacturing concerns producing standard products and services.
4. Budgetary control is concerned with a specific period and is based on the totals of amounts. Standard costing is concerned with the standard costs, which are worked out generally per unit of production.
5. Budgetary control is not based on standard costing system. Standard costing cannot exist in the absence of a budgetary control system.

COMPARISON

Physical inventory	Perpetual inventory
1. It is an which is recorded on the basis of regular checks which can be fortnight, weekly, monthly, depending upon the organisation policies.	1. It is maintained a regular basis by concerned department taking into considerating the issues and daily usage.
2. It should be equal to perpetual totals.	2. Perpetual amount digits should be equal to physical totalled amounts.
3. It is a periodic actual record process.	3. It is a continuous actual record process.
4. It is maintained for all the items or products.	4. It is maintained only for selected items.
5. Format used in recording details is physical inventory form.	5. Format used in recording details is perpetual inventory form.

OTHER DEPARTMENT OF STOCK TAKING

- Storage capacity
- Shelf life
- Delivery schedules
- Savings on volume purchasing
- Operating periods
- Volume of sales
- Working capital
- Future availability
- Variety of menus

QUESTIONNAIRE

1. What is inventory control?
2. What are the objectives of inventory control?
3. What are different methods of inventory control?
4. Explain the physical inventory and perpetual inventory method. Draw the formats of forms required to be maintained in different inventory methods?
5. Brielfly explain the tools and techniques used in inventory control?
6. What is zero based budgeting and points to be observed in setting it?
7. What is the role of EOQ in inventory control?
8. How is bin cards useful in controlling inventory?
9. Make the comparison between the physical and perpetual inventory method?
10. List the other departments helpful in inventory control?

UNIT 10

BEVERAGE CONTROL

INTRODUCTION

Beverages, means BOIRE in French means "to drink. They can be classified into alcoholic or non-alcoholic.

Beverage control is very similar to food control in many ways. It is necessary to develop standards and procedures for purchasing, receiving, storage, issuing, production and the sales. Those standards and procedures are like those used in food control, only instead of dealing with highly perishables food items that in many cases it can be kept indefinitely.

DEVELOPING STANDARDS AND STANDARD PROCEDURES FOR PURCHASING

The main objective of establishing beverage purchasing controls is to maintain an appropriate supply of ingredients for producing beverage products, and to ensure that the quality of each is appropriate to its indented use and that each is purchased at the optimum price. The key is the establishment of standards and standard procedures. Standards must be developed for:

1. Quality of beverages purchased.
2. Quantity of beverages purchased.
3. Prices at which the beverages are purchased.
4. Establishing standard procedure for purchasing

1. Establishing Quality Standards: Alcoholic beverages used by a bar can be divided into two classes according to the use ie. ***call brands and pouring brands***. A pouring brand is used whenever the customer does not request a call brand as call brands are normally expensive or can be out of stock and pouring brands are easily available at a particular place.

2. Establishing Quantity Standards: The beverage products are not highly perishable if properly stored or used, beverages can be purchased far less frequently as of perishable foods. The principal factors used to establish quantity standards for beverage purchasing are:

- Frequency with which management chooses to place orders
- Storage space available.
- Funds available for inventory purchases.
- Delivery schedules set by purveyors.
- Minimum order requirements set by purveyors
- Price discounts for volume orders.
- Limited availability of some items.

To establish quantity standard for beverages, then, management has to take all of these factors in to account. This is done best by those who have considerable experience with beverage management and are fully informed about all aspects of the beverage operation, including its financial status.

3. Establishing Standards of Prices: Assuming that the quality standards can be established and appropriate purchase quantities are known, the next step is to ensure that all beverage purchases are made at the reasonable low price. The establishment of price standards is somewhat complicated by laws that vary from state to state.

Anyone responsible for purchasing the beverages must be familiar with the laws, restrictions, and industry practices of his particular area. If competitive pricing is the rule, the buyer should clearly take full advantage of the situation. If competition is minimal or non- existent, the buyer must simply accept the fact.

4. Establishing standard procedure for purchasing- Having established standards for purchasing beverages, the next step is to establish standard procedures in the hotels. In beverage purchasing, the need exists for standard procedure to:

- Determine Order Quantities.
- Process Orders.

a) **Determining order quantities:** There are basically two methods for determining order quantities. One, known as the periodic order method, is based on fixed order dates and variable order quantities; the second, the perpetual order method, uses variable order dates and fixed reorder quantities.

i) **Periodic order method:** The periodic order method requires that the order dates fixed so that there are equal operating periods between order dates. Ordering may be done weekly, bi-weekly, or on any other regular schedule as per requirement, depending on the decisions of management with respect to frequency of ordering, storage space of beverages, and budget available for inventory purchases.Having established average consumption during the period to which is added some numbers for uncertain delivery time, increase the sales, gives us the par stock- i.e. the maximum quantity of item that should be on hand at any given time. To determine order quantity

ii) **Perpetual order method-** The perpetual order method is based on the establishment of perpetual inventory system for beverages, requiring the use of perpetual inventory cards on which all purchases and issues are recorded carefully and in timely manner. These are normally maintained in the office away from the beverage store. To use the perpetual order method, several key figures must be kept in mind: ***par stock, reorder print and reorder quantity***. Par stock is the maximum quantityof management.Reorder points is the number of units to which the inventory should decrease before an order is placed, and is equal to the difference between par stock and reorder point plus the number of units consumed between order date and delivery date.

b) **Processing Order:** Whenever practical, it is advisable to establish a purchasing routine that requires formal written purchase orders. In large establishment, formal purchase requests serve as the basis of ordering.

Quantity	Item	Size	Supplier	Unit Price	Total Price
6 cases	Old Crow	750 ml	A&C Suppliers		
2 cases	Beefeater Gin	750 ml	A&C Suppliers		

Requested by:............ .... Approved by:.................... Date:...............

Purchase requests from various departments are consolidated and purchase orders are placed.

RECEIVING CONTROLS

Establishing Standards: The primary goal of receiving control is to ensure that the deliveries received should confirm exactly to orders. This means that deliveries must be compared to orders placed with respect to quantity, quality and price and also the temperature. The standards established for receiving are quite simple.

1. The quantity of an item delivered must be equal to the quantity ordered and it can be differed according to the stock available but should be changed in bill.
2. The quality of an item delivered must be the same as the quality ordered. With wine, this may require verifying vintages or checking bottling dates of wines that are best when young. With beer, it may require checking bottling or canning dates to ascertain freshness. With spirits, as with wines and beers, one would check to be certain that the brand delivered was the same as the brand ordered.
3. The price on the invoice for the item delivered should be the same as the price quoted or listed when the order was placed.
4. Standard procedures must be established to ensure that standards will be met.
5. Maintain a good record of all beverages orders placed and the receiving clerk must have these records available.
6. Remove the record of the order from the file when a delivery arrives and compare it to the invoice presented by the delivery driver to verify that quantities, qualities and prices on the invoice to confirm the order.

BEVERAGE RECEIVING REPORT

In many establishments, a beverage receiving report is filled out daily by the person responsible for receiving beverages. It summarizes the invoices for all beverages received on a given day, indicates both quantities received and their values and provides columns for dividing purchases into essential categories- wines, beers, spirits and mixers- for purchase journal distribution.

HOTELS ABC

BEVERAGE RECEIVING REPORT (WEEKLY)

Week ending March 9 Date ____________

Supplier	Liqueur	Wine	Beer	Invoice Total
Atlantic Brewers			221.00	221.00
Shaw Wallace	360.00	440.00		800.00
H&G Agency		200.00		200.00
TOTALS	360.00	640.00	221.00	1221.00

STORING

ESTABLISHING STANDARD

Storing control is established in beverage operations in order to achieve several important objectives.

1. To prevent pilferage.
2. To ensure accessibility of the products when ever needed.
3. To maintain product quality.

To prevent pilferage, it's clearly necessary to make all beverage storage areas safely secured. To establish the proper degree of security, access to storage areas must be restricted to authorized individuals. To ensure accessibility of products when needed, the storage facility must be organized so that each particular beverage product can be easily found when needed. To maintain the product quality, each item in the beverage inventory must be stored appropriately: under conditions that will maximize its shelf life.

STORING OF BEVERAGE

Once beverages are received they must be moved immediately to the cellar and a tight level of control maintained at all times. The storage of beverages is ideally separated into five areas as follows.

- Main storage area for spirits and red wine held at temp of 55°F to 60°F.
- A refrigerated area of 50°F for the storage of white and sparkling wines.
- A further refrigerated area of 43°F – 47°F for kegs.
- An area held at temp of 50°F for storage of beers and soft drinks.
- A totally separate area, from those above for the storage of empty bottles, kegs and crates.

CELLAR RECORDS

- **CELLAR INWARD BOOK:** This provides accurate reference to all beverages coming into the seller and posting data for cellar mans bin cards whenever necessary it is useful to check against the perpetual beverage inventory ledger held in the food & beverage control or a/c's office.

HOTEL ABC CELLAR'S INWARD BOOK DATE............					
DATE	BEVERAGE	DELIVERY NOTE/ INVOICE NO.	BIN CARD NO	BOTTLES	HALVES
SIGNATURE OF RECEIVING OFFICER					

SIGNATURE OF RECEIVING OFFICER

- **BIN CARDS:** These are provided for each individual type of beverage & commodities held in stock and record all deliveries and issue made. The card being fixed on the shelves or racks against each beverages and commodity, showing date, quantity of goods received, quantity of goods, bin card no. referring to the same bin no. as the wine list originated from the standard bottle code list.This helps in hanling beverages and commodities.

HOTEL ABC BIN CARD BIN NO: BOTTLE SIZE TYPE: WHITE HORSE WHISKEY					
DATE	ITEMS	RECV	ISSUED TO BAR A B C	TOTAL	BALANCE

- **CELLAR CONTROL BOOK:** This provides control of all daily deliveries to the cellar and the daily issue of each beverage from the cellar to the various bars and should cross check with the entries on the bin card and perpetual inventory, ledger held in control or accounts office.
- **BEVERAGES PERPETUAL LEDGER:** This master ledger, which is prepared in control or a/c's office, consists of cards prepared for each individual type of beverages held in stock.
- **ULLAGE AND BREAKAGE:** It is necessary for any breakage to be recorded on a standard form together with an explanation and countersigned by a member of the food and beverage department.

- **COMPLIMENTRY BOOK:** This is necessary to record the issue of drink to the kitchen and other grades of staff as laid down by the company's policy.
- **EMPTY RETURN BOOK:** The supplier against a delivery charges many of the containers of beverages such as crates, kegs, etc. A counter record book should be maintained, which records all container received from the various suppliers

CELLAR CONTROL BOOK

BIN CODE NO.	ITEM	UNIT	OPEN STOCK	ISSUE	TOT	RETURN	BAL STOCK	BAL BY STOCK TAKE	VARIANCE	VALUE ISS AT COST	VALUE OF BAL AT COST

ESTABLISHIN-G PAR STOCK

As used in bar operations, the meaning of the item par stock is somewhat different. In store room operation par stock means the maximum quantity that may be on hand at any time; it's a limit which a quantity on hand should never exceed the given quantity. In bar operations par stock is the precise quantity stated in numbers of bottles or other containers, which must be at hand on all times for each beverage at the bar.

REQUISITION SYSTEM FOR ISSUING

A requisition system is a highly structured method for issuing goods. In beverage control.

BEVERAGE REQUISTION BAR DATE						
S.NO	BIN #	QTY	UNIT	ITEM	C.P UNIT TOTAL VALUE	S.P UNIT TOTAL VALUE
RECV BY REQUISTIONED BY						

A key element in the system is requisition form, on which both the beverages are issued and the quantities are recorded. No bottles should ever be issued without a written requisition signed by an authorized person.

BEVERAGE PRODUCTION CONTROL

Beverage production control is based on establishing quantity standards.

DEVICES FOR MEASURING

1. Short glass- plain and lined.
2. The Jigger.
3. The pourer.
4. Automated dispenser.
5. Free pour.
6. Glassware.

Standard recipes for mixed drinks help to standardize portion cost. For straight drinks the standard portion cost is determined as:

STANDARD OUNCES IN THE BOTTLE

This gives no. of portion per bottle. Cost per bottle divide by no. of portions gives cost per portion. Standard selling prices should be determined for each drink and each outlet.

MONITORING BEVERAGE OPERATIONS

There are 3 general approaches to measure the effectiveness of the beverage controls. The decision of which to use depends on the size and scope of operation, and as well as management philosophy. The first is based on determination of cost of beverages sold and comparison of that figure with either actual cost or standard cost. The 2nd based on liquid measure A: Comparison of the number of ounces of beverages sold with the number of ounces of beverages consumed. The 3rd in based on sales value: comparison of potential sales value of beverages comparison with the actual sales revenue recorded. Many operators use just one of these methods; some use more than one.

1. The cost approach
2. Cost percent methods
3. Monthly calculations

It's useful to compare cost and sales figures on a regular basis to see if the anticipated cost-to-sales is being maintained.

A physical inventory of storage area is taken, usually immediately after the close of business on the last day of the month. The number of bottles of each item in stock is counted and its value in determined

Cost percentage = Cost/ Sales.

ADJUSTMENTS TO COST

Food and beverage transfers have the following effects:

Add: Cost of food for the garnishes transferred to bar

Add: Cost of mixers.

Less: Cost of beverage issued to kitchens Cost of drinks served to officers. Cost of drinks served as promotion.

To calculate the standard cost for a given operating period, one needs record for the number of sales of each specific period. For e.g.: the record of the spirit sales have to show type of drink and brand of liquor. Types of drinks include cocktails, mixed drinks & straight shots. Record of beer sales would have to show both bottle sales and draft sales by brand. Equivalent detail records of wine sales would also be needed.

THE LIQUID MEASURE APPROACH/OUNCE- CONTROL METHOD: Another technique for beverage control is the quantity control or ounce control method. Some years ago it involved taking daily physical inventory of bar stock in order to determine the no. of ounces consumed and calculating for detailed sales records the number of ounces sold. Ideally the no. of ounces consumed should equal the no. of ounces sold; in practice, they never do equal one another because of spillage, evaporation and breakage. However when the bar is operated carefully, paying strict attention to the standard set by, management, the difference can be kept to minimum.

SALES VALUE APPROACH: If a standard drink of gin is 1 ounce, and gin is issued in 1 lit bottle, then each bottle potentially contains 33.8 drinks. If the standard drinks sell for Rs.35 then, the sale value of bottle would be 33.5 × 35 = 1172.50. This is the value that each bottle of gin sold should recover.

However this applies to straight drink. In the case where cocktails and mixed drinks are sold some way must be found to account for the differences that arises form the production of mixed drinks.

ACTUAL SALES VALUE: It is possible where detailed sales records are available where the value of ingredients of each drink can be calculated.

STANDARD DEVIATION METHOD: This approach requires the establishment of test period during which management takes all appropriate steps to ensure strict adherence to all standards and procedures. In addition the bar operations are kept under strict observation. Bottle consumption is translated to potential sales value of each bottle. A potential sales value is determined that indicates what the total sales value might have been if all the sprits consumed had been by straight drinks. Next actual sales are compared with potential sales. The difference is attributed to mix drinks and spillage. This difference is taken as the standard difference. This difference is dividing by potential sales to given a percentage. By reducing the potential sales figure by this percentage helps to arrive at what might be the reasonable actual sales.

BAR FRAUD: Individual or set of tasks done with a mal intention to mislead or misrepresent the management / guest or to generate a financial benefit for the individual doing the fraud. An able manager and a controller keep a constant monitoring arrangement to check any possible chance of frauds. MIS does play an important role in the control procedure.

SOME COMMON FRAUDS

Under Pouring: In this type of fraud the pouring of the drink is intentionally done less than the required quantity. The balance excess alcohol may be sold later. This type of fraud is particularly dangerous as this may lead to quality and quantity variation for the guest as well. It can be prevented by constant and surprise monitoring by the manager. Daily opening and closing inventory of the liquor stock and tallying the sales.

Over pouring: In this kind of fraud there is an intentional pouring of extra measure of drink then the specified one as matter of personal favoritism or ignorance resulting shortage. It can be prevented by correct SOP and strict control.

Substitution: Intentional replacement of a costlier variety with a cheaper one, with similar nature. This often results serious guest complaints. It can be prevented by Guest feedback form analysis and quality check.

Dilution: Diluting liquor with water or any other substance after using part of liquor for some unauthorized interest. It can be prevented by Guest feedback form analysis and quality check. Surprise check.

Non-projected sale: Food and beverage sold under a fraud KOT and bill or an already paid KOT and bill. It can be prevented by strict vigilance and proper channel of F&B control.

QUESTIONNAIRE

1. What are the different standards and procedures for purchasing the beverages?
2. What are the different standards and procedures for receiving the beverages?
3. What are the different standards and procedures for storing the beverages?
4. What are the different standards and procedures for issuing the beverages?
5. What are the different Approaches used in monitoring beverages operations?
6. What are the different methods of controlling beverage operations. How is standard recipe and standard portion used in beverage control?
7. What are the different kinds of frauds in bar and beverage operations?
8. List and draw the formats of various kind of forms, sheets, receipts, registers and reports maintained in books for records in controlling beverage operations.

UNIT 11

SALES CONTROL (MANAGEMENT)

CASH CONTROL

Cash control is a process that is utilized to verify the complete nature and accurate recording of all the cash that is received as well as any cash disbursements that take place. As a broad principle of responsible financial accounting, cash control is introduced where goods and services are bought and sold. As such, businesses, non-profit organizations and households all employ the basic tenets of cash control.

To understand cash control, it is helpful to understand what is meant by cash, when it comes to financial accounting. Along with referring to currency and coin, cash is also understood to include forms of financial exchange like money orders, credit card receipts, and checks. Essentially, any type of financial exchange that can be immediately negotiated for a fixed value qualifies as cash.

Cash control means competently managing all these types of financial instruments by maintaining a perfect tracking system that accounts for both receiving and disbursing the cash. Designing a cash control process is not difficult at all. There are a few basic elements that will be incorporated into the process regardless of whether the cash control procedure is used in the home or in an office or business environment.

PROCEDURE FOR CASH CONTROL

1. Firstly, all the transactions related to cash must be documented and recorded immediately. With cash control, there is no use of the accrual method of accounting. Each cash receipt is recorded upon reception, while each disbursement is entered at the time that the payment is released. The mode of the documentation requires only some of the basic template that will record the necessary data. For the home, a

checking account can be used to track all cash deposited into a common account for the good of the home, with the check book register can serve as the basic document that keeps track of the inbound and outbound transactions.

2. Cash control procedures requires that there should be only certain individuals who have access to the cash and accounts related to cash. This type of security serves two purposes. First, accountability is established for the way that the cash is managed. Second, the empowerment of two people to oversee cash control helps to ensure that important transactions can take place at any given time, even if one individual is unavailable for some reason and the other can handle cash easily.
3. Last, cash control demands that the documents related to the task are kept separated from the physical location of the cash. In other words, the accounting book that is used to record the cash transactions should not be kept in the safe with the currency, money orders, and checks. This simple precaution helps to ensure that the task of altering the physical evidence related to cash in hand is more difficult and thus minimizes the chances for theft to occur.

(Price Look Ups) and department keys accommodate a variety of merchandise items. This means a faster, more accurate check out process and the ability to manage a wider variety of goods and services more efficiently. And with features like fast, attractive receipt print outs and an easy-to-view LCD operator display. The features of the project is given below.

- Fast & Neat Billing with Accuracy
- Easy to use keyboard/alpha numeric backlit display.
- Extensive daily report.
- Day/date/year & precise time with AM/PM.
- Full inventory control.
- Single key Last bill printing
- User programmable Greeting messages.
- Password protection.
- 4-line 20 characters per line backlit LCD.
- Large LED customer display
- PC keyboard for easy operation.
- 999 price look-ups (PLU) for programming automatic price entry
- 10 BPM (Bills Per Minute)

PRE-CHECKING SYSTEM

These machines printed the checks that has to be presented by the server to get the food items. They also kept a running total of items and total sale in monetary unit for each server. They added the extra step, which slowed the waiter down and were new to most waiters. They have added the extra complexity to the operations.

With advent of POS register or pre checking terminals, the delays were eliminated by using remote kitchen production printer which printed the order in kitchen area. Preset keys (a key which will handle the details of menu items), PLU keys (which expands preset keys using pre designated numbers to call up menu items), and price aid in this.It is of 2 types i.e. automated or non automated.

Firstly its the manual i.e. nonautomated.

PROCEDURE:

1. The order is taken by waiter on paper.
2. The waiter sets up account at pre checking terminals, entering the waiters ID number, the number in the party, table number, and a number assigned to the account.
3. The guest check is inserted into the printer and menu items and their cost are recorded.
4. These menu items are also printed at the same in the kitchen which can also print waiter number, time, date and number of people in the party.
5. If additional items are ordered, they can be added later to the check, the check printer can pick up the account number and previous balnc.
6. At the end of meal, the host receives the check automatically totaled with sales tax.

Payment is recorded before the check account number is closed.

Types of Restaurant Check in Automated System

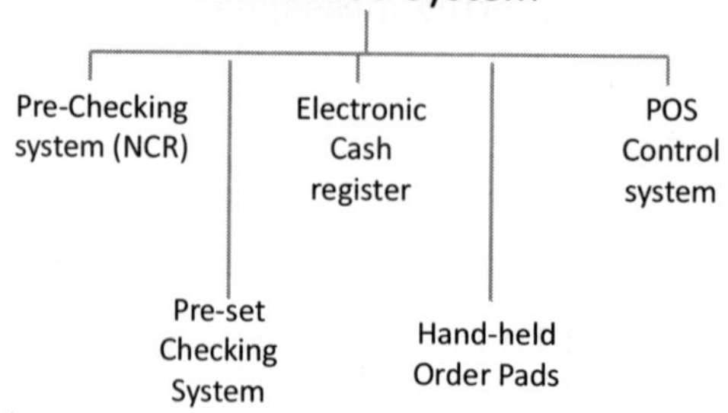

ECR

Electronic Cash Register, High speed machines to record cash transactions in fast service and large volume of catering operations.

A Bill made by Electronic Cash Register

Indian Restaurant
Guest Check/Vat Receipt No.
Server:10 Time:20.30 Table 1/1

1	Bloody Marie	150.00
1	Screw Driver	120.00
2	Seekh Kebab	170.00
2	Mutton Rezalla	200.00
2	Romali Roti	50.00
2	Phirnii	200.00
	Total	890.00
	Taxes 10.5%	93.45
	Paid by Visa	983.00
	Paid by Cash	200.00 TIP

Vat No.: 7896544
Card No. 2010002345

Table No.	Guests	Total Rounded off
8	2	983.00

ECR- ADVANTAGES

1. Price customers' checks through pre-sets or price look-ups.
2. Print checks, including the printing of previously entered items.
3. Have an additional special key so that the pre-set price can be changed during promotional period. E.g. "happy hour in a bar."

4. Produce sales analysis by type of product at any hour of transaction
5. Enable analysis of sales per waiter per hour or per shift period.
6. Analyse sales by method of payment- cash, cheque, type of credit card, etc.
7. Automatic calculations – taxes, service charge, cover charge, etc.
8. Provide limited stock control.
9. Provide waiter checking-in and checking out facility
10. Operator training can be provided without disrupting transaction operation or corruption of information already in the ECR.
11. Restrict access to the ECR and the till drawer by the key or code for each operator.
12. The customer can view the price charged through "turret display". This is advantageous in self service counter and fast food outlet operations.
13. Eliminates the need for cashier. Each waiter becomes responsible for collecting the payment and paying in the exact amount as recorded by the ECR at end of each shift.

- **ECR: Disadvantages/Constraints/Considerations**

1. Suitability – type of operation
2. Cost – in comparing with other products.
3. Model- up-to date or old.
4. Training to be provided to operate.
5. ECR be linked with other ECRs as a part of network.
6. Maintenance – level/cost/frequency.
7. Safeguards – memory loss when power failure.
8. Restriction of access to commands, re-setting, disclosure of information to any other than authorised persons.
9. Ability to function when near to any other powerful electrical equipment.
10. Ability to restrain entry of moisture/dust/foreign particles that can interfere with the operation of the keys.

NCR

National cash register, it is basically used in semi automated properties which helps the auditor to know the sales of any restaurant outlet. It is easy to handle and good for these type of properties.

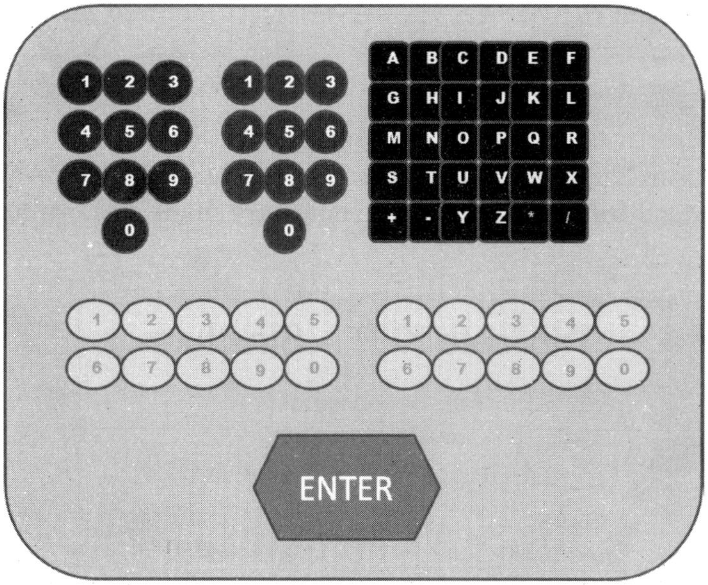

POINT OF SALE (POS): Point of sale (POS) (also sometimes referred to as Point of purchase (POP)) or checkout is the location where a transaction occurs. A "checkout" refers to a POS terminal or more generally to the hardware and software used for checkouts, the equivalent of an electronic cash register. A POS terminal manages the selling process by a salesperson accessible interface. The same system allows the creation and printing of the receipt.

Hospitality point of sales systems are computerized systems incorporating registers, computers and peripheral equipment, usually on a computer network. Like other point of sale systems, these systems keep track of sales, labor and payroll, and can generate records used in accounting and book keeping. They may be accessed remotely by restaurant corporate offices, troubleshooters and other authorized parties.

Point of sales systems have revolutionized the restaurant industry, particularly in the fast food sector. In the most recent technologies, registers are computers, sometimes with touch screens. The registers connect to a server, often referred to as a "store controller" or a "central control unit." Printers and monitors are also found on the network. Additionally, remote servers can connect to store networks and monitor sales and other store data

The efficiency of such systems has decreased service times and increased efficiency of orders.

Another innovation in technology for the restaurant industry is Wireless POS. Many restaurants with high volume use wireless handheld POS to collect orders which are sent to a server. The server sends required information to the kitchen in real time.

REPORTS

1. **K.O.T.:** Kitchen order ticket, it is used by the waiter to give in kitchen, to take food from the kitchen, 3 copies are made, also called triplicate system.

Triplicate KOT – Structure

Logo

NAME OF ORGANISATION
NAME OF THE OUTLET

KOT NO..................

TABLE NO.......... TIME...........
WAITER NO........... NO. OF COVERS

QUANTITY DESCRIPTION

DATE SIGNATURE

2. **RESTAURANT SALES SUMMARY SHEET:** These are basically of all the outlet including all types of sales their charges, taxes and other required information.

Luncheon Service														Date: 23/12/2007	
Bill No.	Waiter No.	Table No.	No. of Covers	Room No.	Amount Paid			Food	Still Room Beverages	Soft Drinks	Beer and Wines	Liqueur spirit	Tobacco	Taxes	Total
					Cash	Credit Card	Signed								
031		2	4		1020			700			220			100	1020
032		5	2	305			450	250				100	50	50	450
033		11	8			4000		2500			200	300		500	4000
034		6	5	214			1150	650				350		150	1150
035		4	3			3000		1200	120	200	400	400	200	480	3000
				TOTAL	1020	7000	1600	5300	120	200	820	1650	250	1280	9620
						9620					9620				9620

3. **RESTAURANT CHECK:** This is prepared by waiter to pick up food and in case this is lost the waiter has to pay Rs. 1000 as compensation in terms of fine.

Logo & Name of the Organisation

Bill

No. Food/XXXX
Wine/XXXX

KOT No. Room No.
Waiter No. Table No.
Name of the Outlet

Quantity	Description	Rate	Amount	
			Rs.	P.
		Total S. Charge S. Tax		
		Grand Total		

VAT No. Slogan of the Organisation

....
Cashier
E & O E

Customer's Copy

....

Received Rs............................ P..... from Waiter No...............for service against KOT No............. Bill No............. at Table No...............

Cashiers signature and Seal

(Cashier's copy)

Received Rs............................ P..... from Waiter No...............for service against KOT No............. Bill No............. at Table No...............

Cashiers signature and Seal

(Waiter's copy)

THEFTS

To control thefts:

1. Proper auditing should be done
2. Security should be provided with good budget
3. Suspicious character should be noticed properly
4. Physical Verification of inventory as per schedule
5. Usage at events should be checked
6. All managers and executives must perform well interms of thefts as this need cleverness.
7. Security should be alerted if in case of any theft
8. G.M. should also be informed.
9. At last if required call the police
10. If the matter is resolved and guest is satisfied then no need to call the police.

CASH HANDLING

1. Cash handling must be properly briefed and encouraged to do it well
2. The Bank Recouncillation Statement should be prepared on regular basis
3. Payment should be preferably paid by cheques
4. Cash and bank cheque must be safely handled
5. Salary must be paid by direct payment
6. Attendence must be verified before giving salary
7. 2 or 3 must sign large payments
8. Cash book must be up to date and very well audited

QUESTIONNAIRE

1. What is budget and different types of budget?
2. What are the objectives of budget?
3. What is budgetary control?
4. What are the steps in setting a budgetary control?
5. What are the various stages in budget development?
6. What is zero based budget?
7. Explain master budget?
8. Briefly explain the different important budgets to be observed or maintained in controlling resources of an organization?
9. How is the different calculations of ratios helps in budgetary control?
10. What are the different kinds of expenses to be controlled through budgets?

UNIT 12

BUDGETARY CONTROL

DEFINITION

Budget is a financial and/or quantitative statement, prepared and approved prior to a defined Period of time of the policy to be pursued during that period for the purpose of attaining a given objective. It may include income, expenditure and employment of capital.

Budget is an estimate of the incomes and expenses for a given period in the future. It is prepared by the departmental heads and the controller as a guiding tool for future operation. An operating budget plan is a plan that estimates how much income will be generated and what expenses will be incurred to meet investment and profit requirements. Budgets are planning and control tools because they forecast the profits expected in the fiscal period. Once developed budgets become an important part of the control process. Corrective action can be taken on a timely basis on comparison with plans.

Budgetary control involves:

1. Setting objectives and goals.
2. Dividing the business and work into various responsibility centers for preparing various budgets.
3. Recording actual figures and facts.
4. Comparing actual budget with last one.
5. Correct action to correct variation.

OBJECTIVES

1. To ensure planning for the future i.e. to anticipate expected performance.
2. To coordinate the activities of different departments.

3. To operate various cost centers and departments with economy and efficiency.
4. To eliminate waste and increase profitability.
5. To anticipate capital expenditure for the future.
6. To centralize the control system.

TYPES OF BUDGET

Budget may be of various types:

1. Short term
2. Long term
3. Current Cash
4. Capital
5. Operating budget
6. Functional budget
7. Master budget.

STAGES OF BUDGET DEVELOPMENT

1. Forecast of the expected sales income are determined.
2. Required profit levels for food and beverage are calculated.
3. Appropriate method is used to calculate projected costs in generating sales income.
4. Calculate Projected Sales:
   - Sales estimation id based on many factors that include sales histories, identifying trends, current factors, economic variables and other factors.
5. Determine Profit Requirement:
   - Sales income is used for two purpose:
   a) To provide required profits.
   b) To pay for expenses incurred to generate income.
6. Based on the allowance expenses- proper appropriation is done to allocate expenses by extending current levels of expenses. This is usually done by percentage mark up method.

ZERO BASED BUDGET: This method avoids the disadvantages of other methods by starting from zero instead of extending costs or costs percentages. This method takes more time and It involves starting from zero for each category of expenditure. It helps to avoid errors that could have been made in the previous periods or previously inefficient operations.

KEY FACTOR: Budgets of some organization are interdependent on some other budgets. This is called the key factor. For example: the restaurant sale is dependent on number of seats, area, capacity etc.

FRAME WORK: The essential framework for budgeting is as follows:

- Organization for budgeting control.
- Allocation budget centers.
- Budget manual- Duties and responsibilities as far as budget is concerned.
- Budget officer- for co ordination of different areas.
- Period of budget.
- Determining limiting factors. For example: Budget and menu pricing to determine base selling price
    a. Food cost as per budget: 35%
    b. Calculate multiplier: 100/35= 2.86
    c. SP: Food Cost X Multiplier= For e.g. Rs.40 * 2.86= 114.4
    d. Make adjustment for competition, sales mix and tactics.

MASTER BUDGET: Various functional budgets are integrated into master budget. This budget is prepared by the ultimate integration of separate functional budgets. According to ICWA London "the master budget is the summary incorporating its functional budget". Master Budget prepared by the budget officer and it remains with the top level management. This budget is used to co ordinate the activities of various functional departments are used to control the device. Multi unit budgets may be the "bottom up" in which operating budgets ate assembled at the unit level and rolled up the organization or where budgets are made at the corporate level and passed down to lower levels in which it is called "top down". The format of a budget is almost like a P&L statement.

TYPES OF EXPENSES

- Payroll and related
- Cost of Food and Beverage
- Advertising
- Heat, light and power

- Repairs and maintenance
- Replacement of linen, china etc
- Capital improvements
- Operating supplies

BUDGETARY CONTROL

- It refers to the principles, procedures and practices of achieving given objectives through budget.
- It presupposes the existence of a policy.
- Profit target are set.

STEPS FOR BUDGETARY CONTROL

- fixing the objectives and goals
- Laying down an exact and detailed course of action.
- Drawing up the budget by translating the course of action into quantitative and monetary terms.
- Making periodic assessment of the actual result and the achieved results and devising steps to remove losses.

PREPERATION OF THE BUDGET

- Preparation of budget mainly involve two major steps of determination of the profit target and the "limiting factors" depending on which the cost centers devise the budget on the concrete base of policy.

SOME OF THE IMPORTANT BUDGETS TO BE OBSERVED

MASTER BUDGET: This particular budget totals up the entire budget and is worked out in order to check the overall position regarding the volume to be achieved. A higher degree of coordination is required to prepare this.

OPERATING BUDGET: These deals incomes and expenditure of the business. In this yardstick and goals are set for measuring the performance. In revenue producing dept. the target is set in terms of volumes. Later all the operating budgets are consolidated and a P&L statement is prepared.

CASH BUDGET: Although not mentioned earlier in the categorization the cash budget forms an integral part of the system of overall budget.

- The Cash budget predetermines the cash inflow and out flow over a future period.

- Broadly can be calculated in tow parts namely cash receipts and disbursement.
- For cash receipt – an immediate cash source is determined.
- For cash disbursement – food cost, beverage cost etc and other immediate expenses are calculated.

CAPITAL BUDGET: These are related to the capital structure and liquidity of the enterprise. Thus for this, plan of expenditure involving the acquisition, creation or expansion of fixed assets are prerequisites.

CONTROL RATIOS IN BUDGETING

CAPACITY RATIOS: It indicates the extent to which budgeted hours of activity are actually utilized.

$$\text{Capacity Ratio} = \frac{\text{Actual hours worked}}{\text{Budgeted hour}} \times 100$$

ACTIVITY RATIO: Measure of the level of activity attained over a period.

$$\text{Activity ratio} = \frac{\text{Standard hours of actual production}}{\text{Budgeted standard hours}} \times 100$$

EFFICIENCY RATIO: Ratio is an indicator of the degree of efficiency attained in production.

$$\text{Efficiency ratio} = \frac{\text{Standard hours for actual production}}{\text{Actual hours worked}} \times 100$$

CALENDER RATIO: Whether all the budgeted working days in a period have been availed in actual practice.

$$\text{Calender ratio} = \frac{\text{No. of actual working days}}{\text{No. of working days in the Budgeted period}} \times 100$$

QUESTIONNAIRE

1. How is cash controlled in sales operation?
2. What is the prodecure of cash control?
3. How is machine system useful in controlling sales?

4. How does the machines like ECR and NCR used in controlling cash and sales operations?
5. What does it mean by POS and how is hospitality point of sales system useful?
6. What are the various reports formed and maintained in sales operations?
7. List the various kinds of thefts and frauds that may occur in sales control?
8. How is cash handled in sales operations?

UNIT 13

VARIANCE ANALYSIS

DEFINITION

The main difference between standard and actual is known as variance and the detailed analysis of the factors that are influencing such differences and finding remedial solution to eliminate undesirable differences is known as variance analysis.

A variance is said to be ideal when the actual cost is less than the standard and unfavorable when it exceeds the standard cost.

STANDARD COST

It refers to the expectation costs under anticipated conditions. Standard cost systems allow for comparison of standard versus actual costs. Differences are directly referred to as standard cost variances. Variances should be strictly investigated if significant. Standard costs are developed in a number of ways:

a. Specified by the formulas or the recipes.
b. Developed from the price lists provided by suppliers.
c. Determined by time and motion studies are to be conducted industrial engineers.
d. Developed from analyses of past data from previous years.

IDEAL VERSUS ATTAINABLE STANDARDS

1. **Ideal standards (perfection standards):** These are developed under the assumption that no obstacles to the production process will be encountered.
2. **Attainable Standards:** These are developed under the assumption that there will be an occasional problem in the production process.

TYPES OF VARIANCE

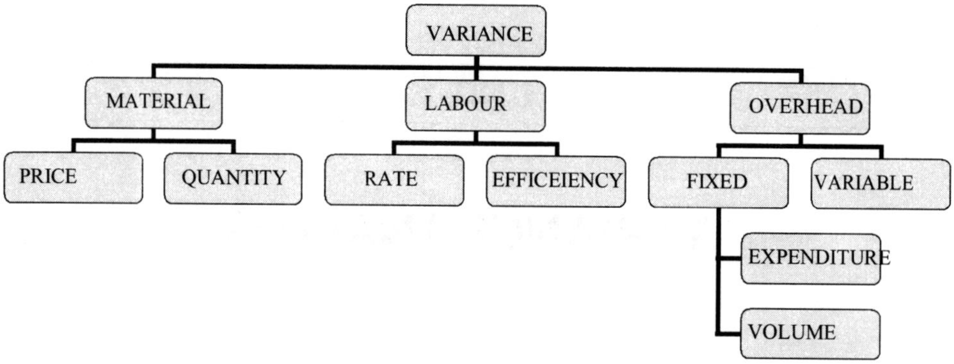

Material Variance: The differences between standard and actual material costs. It is of two types.

a. Material price variance.

b. Material quantity variance.

Reason for Material price variance:

- Fluctuation in market price.
- Inefficient buying.
- Emergency purchase.
- Pricing policies.
- Frauds
- Inappropriate SOP. Department Responsible – Purchase

Material price variance: (AP – SP) × AQp

Where

(AP) = Actual price per unit of material.

(SP) = Standard price per unit of direct material.

(AQp) = Actual quantity of material purchased.

Actual price > standard price: unfavorable.

Actual price < standard price: favorable.

Reason for Material Quantity Variance

- Lack of care while in use.
- Excessive wastage.

- Defective material.
- Poor quality.
- Incorrect specification.
- Lack of training.
- Difference in quality.
- Lack of supervision.
- Defective production. Department Responsible – Store/Purchase

Material quantity variance: (AQu – SQ)SP

Where

(AQu) = actual quantity of material used.

(SQ) = standard quantity of material allowed.

(SP) = standard price of material.

Actual quantity > standard quantity: unfavorable. Actual quantity < standard quantity: favorable.

Labour rate variance – Possible Reasons

- Selecting wrong grade of workers.
- Overtime for urgent reasons.
- Change in basic wage rate.
- Higher rate for quality.
- Seasonal demands.

Department Responsible – Personnel

The rate of labour depends upon the labour time and wage rate.

Labour rate variance (total) = (actual hours × actual rate) – (standard hours X standard rate)

Labour rate variance = (actual rate – standard rate) X actual hours

Labour Efficiency Variance – Possible Reasons

- Defective material.
- Lack of supervision
- Poor working condition.
- Break down
- Power failure

- Change in production method.
- Lack of skill
- Labour turnover
- Discontent

Responsible Department – Individual Department / Personnel

Labour Efficiency variance = (actual hours – standard hours) X standard rate.

Expenditure Variance- Possible Reasons

- Inflation in price level.
- Inefficient control
- Advance payment
- Outstanding payment

Responsible Department – Purchase / Individual Department / Sales.

Overhead Variance- Possible Reasons

- Inefficiency
- Inexperienced labour
- Different material
- New tools
- Operational changes
- Lack / rush of order
- Breakdown
- More or less working days
- Supply delay
- Power supply.

Responsible Departments – Individual Departments / Personnel / Sales / Purchase.

YEAR

Overhead variance = actual overhead cost - (standard hours for the actual output X standard overhead allotted rate)

SALES PRICE VARIANCE

It is difference to profit caused by a change in the selling price of individual unit.

Sales price variance = (standard selling price – actual selling price) X actual sales quantity.

POSSIBLE REASONS

- Unexpected variance
- Rise in price level
- Less quantity of production

Responsible Departments–Sales / Individual Department.

SALES VOLUME VARIANCE

It is the difference to profit caused by a change in the number of units sold.

Sales volume variance = (standard sales quantity – actual sales quantity) X gross profit per unit.

FOOD AND BEVERAGE VARIANCE

The variance analysis which is particular for the F & B Service department can be divided broadly into

1. Sales based variance
   - Sales price
   - Sales volume
2. Cost based variance
   - Food usage
   - Food price
   - Yield standard

FOOD USAGE VARIANCE

This is a check for the quality of food

Food usage variance = (actual quantity – standard quantity) X standard price

FOOD PRICE VARIANCE

Food price variance = (actual price – standard price) × quantity

FOOD YIELD VARIANCE

One of the most important variance as this deals with the portion size and is one of the major criteria for deciding the price. It is a deciding criterion for food quality

Food yield variance = (actual yield – standard yield) X standard cost per output.

QUESTIONNAIRE

1. What is variance analysis?
2. What does it mean by standard cost and standard costing?
3. List and draw a flow chart showing the different kinds of variances?
4. What is material variance and what are the reasons of material quantity and material price variance?
5. What is labour variance and what are the reasons of labour rate variance and labour efficiency variance?
6. What is overhead variance and what are the reasons affecting overhead variance?
7. What is sales variance?
8. What is profit analysis?

UNIT 14

BREAKEVEN ANALYSIS

DEFINITION

- It is very common for food and beverage mangement to be faced with problems concering the levels of f&b cost that can be affected, the prices that need to be set for f&b. Break even analysis enables the relationship between fixed, semi-fixed variance costs at specific volume of business to be conveniently represented on a graph.
- The break even point is the point where the gains equal the losses. The point defines when an investment will generate a positive return. The point where sales or revenues equal expenses. The point where total costs equal total revenues. There is no profit made or loss incurred at the break even point. It is the lower limit of profit when prices are set and margins are determined.
- At this point the income of the business exactly equals its expenditure. If production is enhanced beyond this level, profit shall accrue to the business and if it is decreased from this level, loss shall be suffered by the business.
- A Break Even Chart shows in graphic form the relationship between the volumes of business produced (No. of Meal sold) and resulting sales income, expenditure and profit or losses. In doing so it shows at what sales volume the operation will cover its expenses and begin making a profit.
- In can portray the anticipated effect of menu price changes. It could help determine whether higher menu price would more than offset a predicted lower customer volume or lower menu price could be balanced by customer increase.

- Sales and cost categories are shown in graphic form on Break-Even Chart. It allows to see preplanned cost for any volume. By indicating profit and sales, it encourages concentration on profit and sales.
- Potential financial troubles may be revealed before they are incurred, allowing action to be taken before a problem an arise rather than it has eaten into some profit. The portrayal of cost and sales in graphic form makes it easier for some to assimilate the information than if it had been presented in conventional tabular or statistical form.
- A Break- Even- Chart may be used to illustrate previous performance or it may be prepared as budget or a forecast of future performance. The figure expressed in a break even chart can be used in planning control and decision making.
- The relationship can also be helpful in understanding how all cost must be covered in menu pricing. Involved in these relationships is the contribution to overhead and profit or contribution ratio.

PV RATIO

The relationship between contribution and sales could be expressed in terms of PV ratio.when the variance cost are divided by sales we get variable cost ratio. If variable cost is subtracted from, we get the PV ratio.

$$\text{Contribution ratio} = 1 - \frac{\text{vc}}{\text{sales}}$$

Comparison of PV ratio of different dishes on menu can be made to find out which one is more profitable.

Higher the ratio, higher the profits and vice-versa.

$$\text{PV Ratio} = \frac{\text{sales} - \text{vc}}{\text{sales}} \times 100$$

CONTRIBUTION

In a operation, it is possible to determine sales volume needed to cover given fixed cost of unit sales price and variable cost per unit is available for analysis.the difference between sales value amd marginal cost of sales.each cover is required to contribute to a fund which is the total of all fixed overheads, the balance, if any, is the profit or loss.

MARGINAL COST

This is the cost of producing one more unit of a good or product. Marginal cost is increase or dsecrease in the total cost of a production run for making one additional unit of an item. It is thus the aggregate of direct material, direct wages, direct expense and variable overhead.

PREPARING A BREAK EVEN CHART

The format for break even chart is an L-shaped. Usually the vertical line on the left is used to indicate sales amount in dollar / rupee and horizontal bottom line indicate the no. of unit or meals sold.

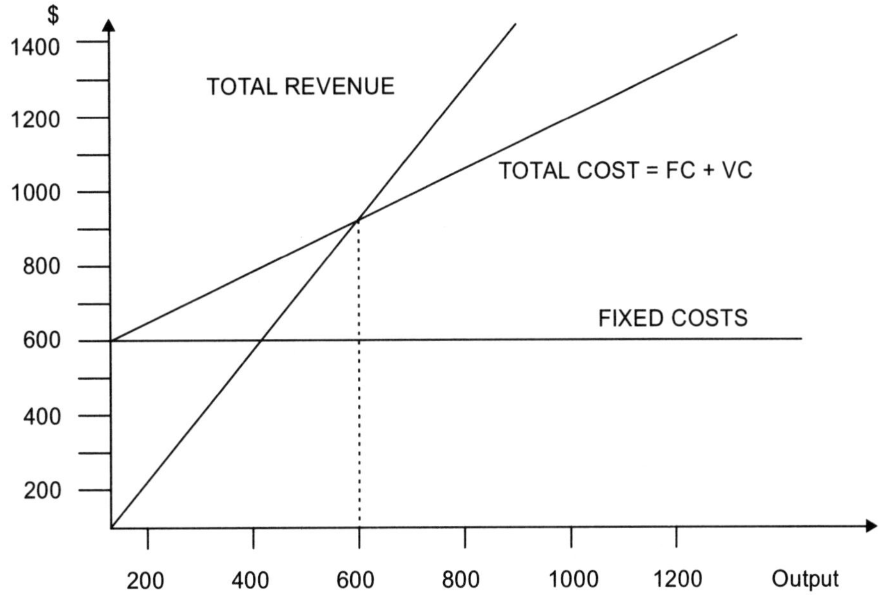

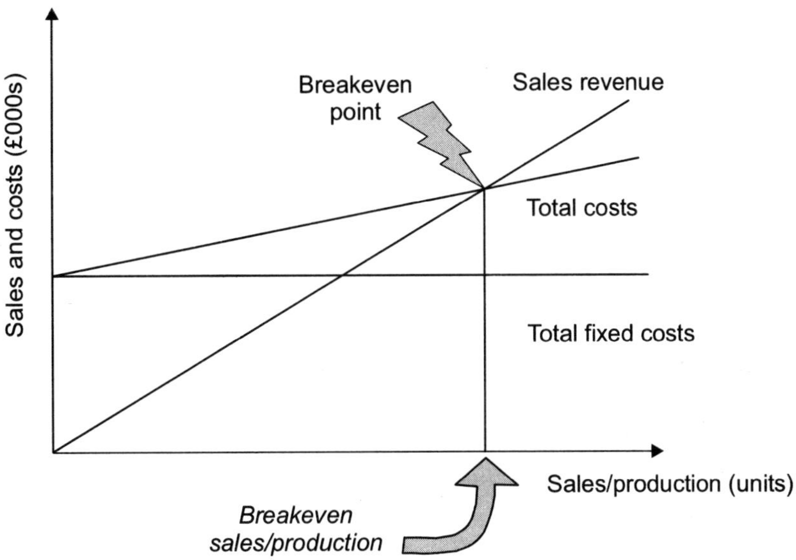

GRAPH

- Breakeven chart
- Profit Volume Chart

Example

Units Sold = 120,000
Per Unit Selling Price = Rs. 1
Per Unit Variable Cost = Rs. 0.50
Fixed Cost = Rs. 40,000

Income Statement

Sales	120,000
Less Variable Cost	60,000
Contribution Margin	60,000
Less Fixed Cost	40,000
Profit	20,000

CONVENTIONAL BREAKEVEN CHART

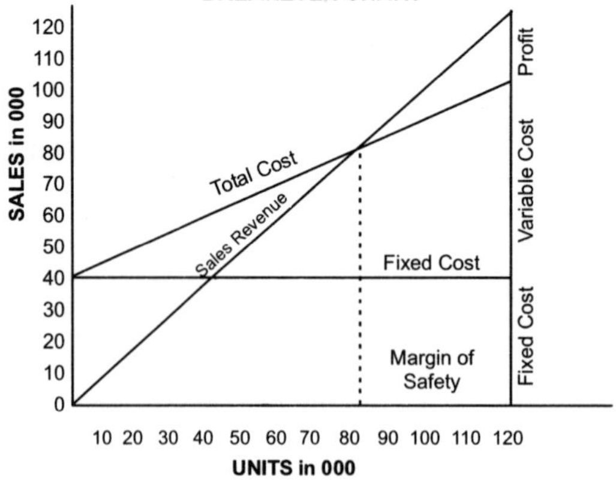

CALCULATION OF BREAK EVEN POINT

Break even point is the level of sales at which profit is zero. According to this definition, at break even point sales are equal to fixed cost plus variable cost. This concept is further explained by the following equation:

(Break even sales = fixed cost + variable cost)

The break even point can be calculated using either the **equation method** or **contribution margin method**. These two methods are equivalent.

Equation Method: The equation method centers on the contribution approach to the income statement. The format of this statement can be expressed in equation form as follows:

Profit = Sales "Variable expenses" Fixed expenses

Rearranging this equation slightly yields the following equation, which is widely used in cost volume profit (CVP) analysis:

Sales = Variable expenses + Fixed expenses + Profit

According to the definition of break even point, break even point is the level of sales where profits are zero. Therefore the break even point can be computed by finding that point where sales just equal the total of the variable expenses plus fixed expenses and profit is zero.

Example:

For example we can use the following data to calculate break even point.

- Sales price per unit = Rs 250
- variable cost per unit = Rs 150
- Total fixed expenses = Rs 35, 000

CALCULATE BREAK EVEN POINT

CALCULATION

Sales = Variable expenses + Fixed expenses + Profit 250Q = 150Q + 35, 000 + 0

100Q = 35000 Q = 35, 000 /100 Q = 350 Units

Q = Number (Quantity) of units sold.

The break even point can be computed by finding that point where profit is zero.

The break even point in sales can be computed by multiplying the break even level of unit sales by the selling price per unit.

Break- Even Sales = 350 Units × 250 Per unit = 87, 500

CONTRIBUTION MARGIN METHOD

This may be defined as the excess of revenue of a product over the variable cost of producing it. It is therefore the contribution to the recovery of fixed cost and profit. The contribution margin method is actually just a short cut conversion of the equation method already described. The approach centers on the idea discussed earlier that each unit sold provides a certain amount of contribution margin that goes toward covering fixed cost. To find out how many units must be sold to break even, divide the total fixed cost by the unit contribution margin.

The Unit Contribution Margin (C) is Unit Revenue (Price, P) minus Unit Variable Cost (V):

C = P – V

Break even point in units = Fixed expenses / Unit contribution margin 35, 000 / 100 per unit

350 Units

Unit Contribution Margin = 250 (Sales) — 150 (Variable exp.)= 100 / unit

A variation of this method uses the Contribution Margin ratio (CM ratio) instead of the **unit contribution margin**. The result is the break even in total sales dollars rather than in total units sold.

Break even point in total sales = Fixed expenses / CM per unit 35, 000 / 0.40 = 87, 500

Where

Contribution Margin = 1 – Variable cost per unit/ selling price per unit = 1 – 150/250 = 1 – 0.6 = 0.4

This approach is particularly suitable in situations where a company has multiple products lines and wishes to compute a single break even point for the company as a whole.

The following formula is also used to calculate break even point

Break Even Sales = [Fixed Cost / 1 – (Variable Cost per unit / Selling price per unit)]

This formula can produce the same answer:

Break Even Point = [35, 000 / 1 – (150 / 250)]

= 35, 000 / 1 – 0.6

= 35, 000 / 0.4

= 87, 500

BENEFITS / ADVANTAGES OF BREAK EVEN ANALYSIS

The main advantages of break even point analysis is that it explains the relationship between cost, production, volume and returns. It can be extended to show how changes in fixed cost, variable cost, commodity prices, revenues will effect profit levels and break even points. Break even analysis is most useful when used with partial budgeting, capital budgeting techniques. The major benefits to use break even analysis is that it indicates the lowest amount of business activity necessary to prevent losses.

LIMITATIONS OF BREAK EVEN ANALYSIS

It is best suited to the analysis of one product at a time. It may be difficult to classify a cost as all variable or all fixed; and there may be a tendency to continue to use a break even analysis after the cost and income functions have changed.

REVIEW PROBLEM 1

Voltar Company manufactures and sells a telephone answering machine. The company's contribution format income statement for the most recent year is given below:

	Total	Per unit	Percent of sales
Sales	Rs1,200,000	Rs 60	100%
Less variable expenses	900,000	45	
	--------	--------	--------
Contribution margin	300,000	15	
Less fixed expenses	240,000	======	======

Net operating income	Rs 60,000		
	======		

Calculate break even point both in units and sales. Use the equation method.

Solution:

Sales = Variable expenses + Fixed expenses +Profit 60Q = 45Q + 240, 000 + 0
15Q = 240, 000
Q = 240, 000 / 15 per unit
Q = 16, 000 units; or at 60 per unit, 960, 000

QUESTIONNAIRE

1. What is break even analysis?
2. With the help of diagram and graphic representation show the breakeven point, breakeven analysis and Profit volume chart.
3. How is breakeven point calculated?
4. What is PV Ratio and how it is calculated?
5. What is marginal cost and Contribution?
6. What is contribution margin method?
7. What are the advantages and disadvantages of breakeven analysis?

UNIT 15

MENU MERCHANDISING

DEFINITION

Themenu is the key factor in influencing the guest's first impreesion of the facility, the menu selections they are likely to oeder and sets expectations about food and beverage, they are about to receive.

The term Menu Merchandising refers to the efforts made by the establishment to sell the menu. It also means making the best and most effective use of menus as means of advertising and selling in a hotel.

The success of Catering operations depends to a greater extent on the way, the menus are planned and designed. Menus are the backbone of any Catering Operation. It is the menu which determines or sets the pattern for so many other factors which are important to the operation, in other words the Catering policies are determined by the menu. It is the menu which is made first. The menu should reflect the management policy and thinking. A good menu should ensure profits.The major concern which caterscienc utilise a menu to optimise their sales and incomes.

MENU: A MARKETING TOOL

Menus have a lot of sale value. To make the best or most effective use of menus as a means of advertising and selling is a **menu merchandising**.

It is the piece of advertising which is sure to be read for this reason. Every detail of the menu deserves closest Scrutiny. The menu must fit the market, the facility, the ability of employees if the operation is to succeed. The menu should have merchandising effect it should help you sell what you want to sell more, and it should also help the guest to choose from the menu what he wants without much loss of time and due consideration should be given to the paper on which it is printed, formatand layout etc.

MENU DESIGN

In order to increase the merchandising value of Menus the following points should be considered while *Designing a Menu.*

1. **Clean:** The presentation of dirty, spotted, worn menu is the poorest way to start a meal. We all know that cleanliness is a must in our business. A soiled menu has a very poor merchandising value; it may raise doubt regarding the food being prepared hygienically. Menu with the continuous long use are likely to get soiled. Soiled menus must be changed with new menus. For this reason the menus cards should not be very expensive. If the investment is high you may be reluctant to discard soiled menus. To keep the menus in good conditions the first important thing is that the paper selected should be of reasonably good quality. The cover should be attractive and glazed. The front cover may also be protected by plastic folders. The inner contents should be changed as and when required. It is a very wrong practice to change the prices on the menu with ink.
2. **Legible:** This means that menus should be easy to ready. The type selected should be attractive and easy to decipher. It should be of sufficient size so that most people, including the elderly or those with glasses, can read it with ease. As far as possible the menus should be printed. Type written menus should be avoided. They are invariably carelessly typed with misspelled words and smeared carbon. Menus should be written in double spacing as single spacing causes confusion and overcrowding. Single spacing tends to give a menu the quality of a telephone directory. Clear readability with plenty of wide space is essential. Easy readability is a must, as menus are meant to be read. The managers must see the lighting arrangements at all tables so that menus can be read. Whether they can be read easily or not. Customers are annoyed when menu is indistinct or light so poor that they cannot read it.
3. **Menu Structure / Format:** The format of the menu should suit contents of menu. As far as possible different formats should be used for different meals. (Breakfast, Lunch, Dinner etc). The format of the menu will also depend upon the type of establishment, its standards and nature e.g. hotels, cafeterias, clubs, etc. The menu should not run into many pages. Two pages menu is considered to be good. Many inserts should be avoided. Don't forget to include the hotel address. The back of the menu can be used for wine list. But a separate wine list is more advisable.
4. **Organized:** A menu should be well organized. Similar items should be grouped together and attractive headings may be assigned to the groups.

The purpose of a well organized menu is that the customer should be able to find what he/she wants quickly without reading the entire menu. Most of us start reading anything at the top left to cocktails and appetizers would be best in this position. Try to group all the categories in an easy to find manner like appetizers, sandwiches, salads, entrée, desserts, and beverages.

5. **Restricted Menus:** The menu should be short as far as possible i.e. the number of dishes on the menu should be limited. Keeping long menus is a poor merchandising policy. There are some operators who may believe that more items you have on the menu the more business you will do. But actually it usually works in reverse.

   The following are the ***DISADVANTAGES*** of Very Long Menus:

   - Confuse the customers and make the selection time longer for them.
   - Overburden the kitchen and serving staff.
   - Do not allow the attention of chef towards the presentation and making of the dish.
   - Increased wastage as there will be more leftover.
   - Slow service as a waiter has to wait for a very long time for the customer to make his selection.
   - Create bottlenecks in the preparation and service area.
   - Buying, receiving, storing, etc of the food becomes difficult and more space is required for storage.
   - Hamper the effectiveness of control process.

   It may be well realized that over if the menu has many items there would still be some guests who would ask for something else. The basis of limiting the menu is to learn about the items which are most popular. The man responsible for planning the menus should check from time to time the sale analysis for different dishes and the items which do not sell reasonably should be removed. Limited should not mean no choice or change at all. Establishments that have permanent regular clientèle must change the menus and should provide ample choice.

   Establishments which have more of tourist business and where the customers change they don't need to change menus frequently.

6. **Easy to change:** Even the most carefully planned menus must be changed from time to time. The change may be necessary because of change in prices, need to add or drop some items for a varied variety of reasons. If a menu is hard to change there may be temptations to mark

out items with pencils or pen, write in items, or worst of all scratch out the old prices and write in the new. The changed prices on the menu has a poor merchandising effect. The menu format and design should be such so that it can be changed with the needs of time.

7. **Fit the operation:** To serve good food with prompt service, you must have a menu designed to fit the place. It must match the size and kinds of equipments, their capacity, and also the skill of the personnel. Never blindly follow your competitors. Never include any item unless you can effectively prepare sell it.
8. **Merchandising effect:** Design your menu to sell the items you want to sell your specialty, or an item that can be served fast and is profitable. Such items should be tactfully located different type faces can be used to emphasis one item over another or attractive borders can be used to make something stand out. While listing the items the one you want to sell fast can be placed at or near the top, since many people read only until they find an item that appeal to them, rather than studying the entire list. Suggest proper cocktails or drinks with a particular food.
9. **Language:** Many a guests are embarrassed to ask what a foreign term means and will pass on to something that they understand where a menu is written in French, the English equivalents should be given. It is a good idea to describe the dishes in the language which is understood by the majority of guests.
10. **Effective description and descriptive headings:** Descriptive headings means quoting such headings on the menu various groups of food which will attract the attention of the customer and will indicate the nature of dish more clearly. The headings assigned to different groups should be interesting and should capture the imagination of the guests.

SOME EXAMPLES

- Sea Coast Delights
- Gourmet Selection
- From The Sizzling Platter
- Oyster Bar
- Dessert Delicacies
- Broiled To Your Order
- Chef's Specials

The explanation of dishes in detail should be avoided, but a brief description should help the customer in making a prompt and suitable selection. Dishes should be described in such a way that a common customer should be able to understand how he is going to get his food and should be able to visualize it. The aim of the description should be to inform the guest regarding the form of food served (method of cooking, cut, hot or cold, etc).

A careful thought given by the person in-charge of making the menu regarding the description, location and the inclusion and omission of certain words help considerably in making a menu worth. It is a good merchandising policy to add extra you are giving to the customer for example instead of writing simply as ***'fillets of sole bonne femme'*** it is better to feature it as ***'fillets of sole bonne femme' served in white sauce with fresh mushrooms and potato borders'.***

Such a description adds to the value of dish. The inclusion of words "with" and "and" in describing the dish add to the value of dish to the customer. Associating of the names of places of origin in describing the dishes are informative and has better sales appeal.

There are words that should be sparingly used on the menu as they are uninviting and lack sales appeal. These are plain, boiled, hashed, minced, mashed etc. Instead of writing as plain omelette write as golden or natural. Spinach should be listed as leaf or garden instead of plain. Mashed potatoes can be better listed as whipped or slow flake. Boiled potatoes as natural or as parsley instead of boiled write as poached or steamed.

The association of some words like fresh tender, green, young, spring, new, chilled, special, choice (The word fresh is not exclusively used for vegetables, fruits etc, otherwise customer might think that the food is canned or stored) in describing or featuring the dish on the menu has better merchandising appeal.

- Grilled Spring Chicken
- Tender Meat/Beef
- Fresh Mushrooms
- Tender Lamb Chops
- New Spring Broccoli
- New Potatoes
- Fresh Fruit Salad
- Young Turkey
- Melon Frappé

- Chilled fruit
- New (Bermuda potatoes, cabbage vegetables)
- Green (peas, cabbage, apple, olives)
- Young (chicken, vegetables, turkey, lobster, beets, carrots)
- spring (vegetable, chicken, lamb salad, onion)
- Garden (vegetable salad)
- Tender (young carrots, buttered beet baby spring lamb chops, roast spring lamb).

MENU PRICING

The pricing of menu is "art of pricing". The successful management analyses the food cost and other overheads, the guests ability to pay for the menu and competitors menu pricing before fixing the menu and its prices. Usually the menus are priced by the General Manager, Chef, Food and Beverage Manager, Sales Manager, Purchase Manager. Each and every factor like food cost, raw material price, competitor's menu price, guest ability to pay, etc. are considered while fixing the price.

FACTORS TO BE CONSIDERED WHILE FIXING THE SELLING PRICE

Some factors involved in menu pricing include:

- **Elasticity of Demand:**

  It means that demand can fluctuate in response to other factors, such as change in pricing, food quality or environment
- **Perception of value:**

  It is what the customer believes the meal worth. You may offer the item with low cost but have relatively high selling price. Different geographical areas or classes of society can have different perception of value. Value is sometimes expressed as quality per price and makes it possible to impose higher prices for prestige and price-sale appeal.
- **Competition:**

  One should constantly aware of what prices are offered by your competitors for same services.
- **Relationship between Menu, Prices and Volume:**

  Two school of thoughts are there you are trying to make small profit per item by selling many items or high profit per item by selling fewer items.

- **Profit in Rupee not Percentage:**

  Many operation stress percentage in their menu pricing. A menu item may very profitable on a percentage basis but because of lower sale it might bring little profit.

- **Total Cost Consideration:**

  In setting their menu price, many operation concentrate primarily on the raw food price involved. Now a days other cost are significant and should be considered.

- **Contribution to profit:**

  Selling price must provide adequate share to fixed cost and other overheads and good margin of profit.

- **Long term implication for pricing:**

  If an operation has reputation of high or low menu price, it can be difficult to change in short run of business. Some commercial operation create financial difficulty for themselves when they try to raise their prices since they have low price reputation or vice- verse.

PRICING METHODS

The menu price fixed should be acceptable to hotel / restaurant and guest. By reducing the price hotel tries to attract more guests and hence try to increase the sale. The large sale reduces the fixed cost per guest and hence hotel makes profit in spite of having a low price. Some hotels may prefer to keep high price and look for high income guests only who can sell more per cover, in spite of having low sale hotel may still make profit. It is very difficult to fix the menu / dish price.

The following are the common pricing methods:

- **The Factor System:**

  This is also known as multiplier or mark up system. The raw food cost (Rfc) is multiplied by pricing factor(Pf) to provide menu selling price (Msp). The pricing factor is determined by dividing desired food cost percentage into 100. If a 40% food cost is desired, dividing 0.40 into 100 will give pricing factor of 2.5.

- **The Prime Cost Factor:**

  The prime cost system considers not only raw food cost but also direct labour cost. Direct labour cost include those cost involved in preparation. It does not include service, sanitation or administrative labour cost then it is multiplied with pricing factor

- **Prime Cost (Pc) = Raw Food Cost (Rfc) + Direct Labour Cost (Dlc)**
- **Prime Cost (Pc) x Pricing Factor (Pf) = Menu selling Price (Msp)**

- **The Actual Pricing Method:**

  This method includes all the cost plus a desired profit to determine the menu selling price.

- **Demand Oriented Perceived Value Pricing:**

  This method is based on the perception of guest and that means what the guest feels after seeing the dish. The price of food matching is perception of ***Value for money. Eg*** The guest in a silver service restaurant is ready to pay than in a self service cafeteria.

- **Price based on Competitor's Price:**

  This is the simplest method of pricing. Here the caterer does not work on cost, profit etc and on the contrary caterer takes pricing of competitor's price as guideline and fixes his price may be slightly higher or lower.

- **Marginal Pricing:**

  The cost can be divided into two categories fixed and variable cost. Usually caterer first aim at getting Break Even Sale. After the BEP any cost which occurs is known as marginal cost and cover the marginal cost and profit is marginal pricing.

- **Gross Profit Method:**

  This method involves in finding gross profit per person and adding price of any extra item to the main meal cost and arriving at the selling price of each menu items.

  - **Selling Price = Cost main item + Accompanying dish + other items cost + GP**

- **Food Cost Method:** In India, it is the most common method of fixing price. Hotel decides to maintain a certain food cost. Before fixing the price, the portion size and the food cost of the dish is calculated. After knowing the food cost then the selling price is decided.

Considerations while planning a menu:

- Types of establishment
- Type of clientele

- Seasonal availability of the raw material
- Capability of the staff members
- Availabilioty of the required equipments
- Pricing of the menu
- Balance of the menu items

Constraints while planning menu:

- Health and eating habits (diet concious)
- Special diets or food items (allergic people)
- Cultural and religious
- Vegetarianism
- Balance of colour, texture, flavours, aroma, garnishing and standard quality, portion size etc.

TYPES OF MENU

Table d'hôte: It means food from the host's table and identified as:

- Being a restricted menu.
- Offering a small number of courses.
- A limited choice within each course.
- A fixed selling price.
- All the dishes being ready at a set time.

These menus can be offered in breakfast, lunch, dinner. Their many adaptations are used for:

- o Banquets
- o Buffets
- o Coffee houses
- o Cyclical menus

Á la carte: It means a free choice from card or menu and is identified by:

- Being usually a larger menu than a Table d'hôte menu and offering a greater choice.
- Listing under the course headings all of the dishes that may be prepared by the establishment.
- All dishes being prepared to order.
- Each dish being separately priced.

- Usually being more expensive than a Table d'hôte menu.
- Often containing the exotic and high cost seasonal foods.

QUESTIONNAIRE

1. What does it mean by menu merchandising?
2. List and explain the points which are considered while designing a menu?
3. What are the factors to be considered while planning a menu?
4. What factors are considered while pricing the menus?
5. What are the different pricing methods used for menus?
6. Which are the points taken care while fixing the selling price?
7. What are the different types of menus?
8. How does the menu act as a marketing tool?
9. What are the constraints in menu planning?

UNIT 16

MENU ENGINEERING

DEFINITION

Menu engineering is a marketting oriented approach to the evaluation of a menu with regards to its present and future content, design and pricing. It is an interdisciplinary field of study devoted to the deliberate and strategic construction of menus. It is also commonly referred to as Menu Psychology.

In general, the term *menu engineering* is used within the hospitality industry (specifically in the context of restaurants), but can be applied to any industry that displays a list of product or service offerings for consumer choice. Typically the goal with menu engineering is to maximize a firm's profitability by subconsciously encouraging customers to buy what you want them to buy, and discouraging purchase of items you don't want them to buy.

METHODS OF MENU ENGINEER

Fields of study which contribute most to menu engineering include:

- Psychology (perception, attention, emotion / effect)
- Managerial Accounting (contribution margin and unit cost analysis)
- Marketing & Strategy (pricing, promotion)
- Graphic Design (layout, typography)

PRE-REQUISITIES FOR USING MENU

- **Standards recipes:** Recipes prepared by the kitchen must be of a standard including presentation, portion size etc.
- **Uniform rate:** The rates of the raw material must be of a standard and uniform prices and quality so that there is no variation in food cost.
- **Sales analysis**: sales analysis of each item must be done daily and by meal period.

- **Computers**: Computers are used for calculating salews, food cost, gross profit, etc. It is recommended that the computers should be used so that all calculations are done accurately and with speed.

PSYCHOLOGY OF MENU ENGINEERING

Perception and Attention: Visual perception is inextricably linked to how customers read a menu. Most menus are presented visually and the majority of menu engineering recommendations focus on how to increase attention by strategically arranging menu categories within the pages of the menu, and item placement within a menu category. This strategic placement of categories and items is referred to as the theory of ***sweet spots.***

The reasoning being Sweet Spots stems from the classical effect in psychology known as the ***Serial position effect***. The thought is, customers are most likely to remember the first and last things they see on a menu - hence, sweet spots on a menu should be where the customers look first and last. To date, there is no empirical evidence on the efficacy of the sweet spots on menus

Customer perception of items offered on a menu can also be affected by subtle textual manipulations. For example, descriptive labeling of item names may produce positive effects, leading to higher customer satisfaction, and higher perceived product value. Similarly, the presence of rupee/ dollar signs or other potential monetary cues may cause guests to spend less.

MANAGERIAL ACCOUNTING

The primary goal of menu engineering is to encourage purchase of targeted items, presumably the most profitable items, and to discourage purchase of the least profitable items. To that end, firms must first calculate the cost of each item listed on the menu. This costing exercise should extend to all items listed on the menu, and should reflect all costs incurred to produce and serve. Optimally item costs should include: food cost (including wasted product and product loss), incremental labor (e.g., cost in in-house butchering, pastry production, or prep), condiments and packaging. Only incremental costs and efforts should be included in the item cost.

After an item's cost and price have been determined, evaluation of an item's profitability is based on the item's ***Contribution Margin.*** The contribution margin is calculated as the menu price minus the cost. Menu engineering then focuses on maximizing the contribution margin of each guest's order. Recipe costing should be updated (at least the ingredient cost portion) whenever the menu is reprinted or whenever items are re-engineered. Some simplified calculations of contribution margin include only food costs.

Date: 10/15/20X2

Restaurant: Midtown Plaza Meal Period: Dinner

A	B	C	D	E	F	G	H	L	P	R	S
Menu Item Name	Number Sold (MM)	Menu Mix %	Item Food Cost	Item Selling Price	Item CM (E-D)	Menu Costs (D-B)	Menu Revenues (E-B)	Menu CM (H-G)	CM Category	MM% Category	Menu Item Classification
1. Beef Stew	350	17.5	4.10	10.00	5.90	1435.00	3500.00	2065.00	Low	High	Plowhorse
2. Chow Mein	210	10.5	4.40	11.25	6.85	924.00	2362.50	1438.50	High	Low	Puzzle
3. Ham Cheese Sandwich	100	5.0	4.80	10.50	5.70	480.00	1050.00	570.00	Low	Low	Dog
4. BLT Sandwich	450	22.5	4.90	12.50	7.60	2205.00	5625.00	3420.00	High	High	Star
5. Hamburger Platter	510	25.5	4.45	11.45	7.00	2269.50	5839.50	3570.00	High	High	Star
6. Chicken Sandwich	380	19.0	2.75	8.50	5.75	1045.00	3230.00	2185.00	Low	High	Plowhorse
Column	N					I	J	M			
Total	2,000					8,358.50	21,607.00	13,248.50			
Additional computations:						K = I/J		O = M/N 6.62	Q = (100%/Items) (70%) 11.7%		

MARKETING (PRICE & PROMOTION)

By using guest demand (also called the menu mix) and gross profit margins, the relative performance of each menu item is determined, and assigned one of the following terms (based on the BCG Matrix).

- **Stars –**

  Stars are extremely popular and have a high contribution margin. Ideally Stars should be your flagship or signature menu items.

- **Plow Horse or Cash Cows –**

  Plow Horses are high in popularity but low in contribution margin. Plow horse menu items sell well, but don't significantly increase revenue.

- **Puzzles –**

  Puzzles are generally low in popularity and high in contribution margin. Puzzle dishes are difficult to sell but have a high profit margin. A menu should have limited puzzles. With low demand, they can lead to production, inventory and cost problem

- **Dogs-**

  Dogs are low in popularity and low in contribution margin. They are difficult to sell and produce little profit when they do sell. They can be eliminated.

  If you want to keep them for a few customer then keep it in A La Carte menu.

In general, items within a relevant comparable set (for example, entrees, or chicken entrees) should be priced to have similar contribution margins - this way, the restaurant would make the same amount of money, no matter what item the guest chooses to order.

BCG (BOSTON CONSULTATION GROUP) MATRIX

Plow horses or Cash Cow High Popularity/ Sale Low Contribution	**Stars** High Popularity/ Sale High Contribution
Dogs Low Popularity/ Sale Low Contribution	**Puzzles** Low Popularity/ Sale High Contribution

ADVANTAGES OF MENU ENGINEERING

- Based on the analysis the caterer can redesign the menu.
- Helps in increasing the profit and reducing losses
- It guides how to face competition.
- It decides the course of marketing.
- Paves the ways for new technology to be used.
- It streamlines the purchasing, storing and production process.
- It determines the staff strength for kitchen and service department.
- It act as tool for marketing for menu.

QUESTIONNAIRE

1. What is menu engineering?
2. what are the objectives of menu engineering?
3. What are the different methods of menu engineering?
4. How does the pshycology factors affects the menu engineering?
5. What is the role of the marketing strategy and graphic designs in menu engineering?
6. What is the benefit of managerial accounting in menu engineering?
7. What are the advantages of menu engineering?
8. Explain the BCG Matrix of menu engineering?

UNIT 17

MANAGEMENT INFORMATION SYSTEM (MIS)

REPORTS

PHYSICAL INVENTORY

- A periodic actual counting of all the products in the storage areas.
- Actual counting is recorded on the basis of checks which can be once a week or a fortnight, a month.
- Physical counting is done before normal opening time or closing time of store or after closing.
- In large organisation, inyventories are taken in parts on weekly basis.
- Inventory process involves atleast two persons- one from controls and other from accounts department.
- One person counts systematically arranged stock and other person records the data on a physical inventory form.
- This form helps in taking physical inventory in shortest possible time.

Physical Inventory Form

S no.	Quantity in hand	Unit size	Food item	description	Unit cost	Total cost

Taken by............... C/F inventory...............

PHYSICAL INVENTORY FORM

PERPETUAL INVENTORY SYSTEM

- Perpetual maintaining a continous records of all purchases and issued items.
- It provides a continous record of goods available on hand at any point of time.
- It is used to restrict the product in the dry and cold or frozen stores.
- It requires a considerable amount of labour to maintain the proper system working.
- It usually used for maintaining selected or expensive items.
- It is necesary to be tallied to physical inventory total amounts at end.

Perpetual Inventory Form (for storeroom)

Item........... **store room...........**

Date	Order No.	Quantity in	Quantity out	Quantity in hand

Perpetual Inventory Form(for bar)

Date	Item	Brought forward	Quantity in	Quantity out	Balance C\F	Remarks

ECONOMIC ORDER QUANTITY - EOQ

DEFINITION OF ECONOMIC ORDER QUANTITY – EOQ:

An inventory-related equation that determines the optimum order quantity that a company should hold in its inventory given a set cost of production, demand rate and other variables. This is done to minimize variable inventory costs. The full equation is as follows:

$$EOQ = \sqrt{\frac{2SD}{PI}}$$

where :

S = Setup costs
D = Demand rate
P = Production cost
I = Interest rate (considered an opportunity cost, so the risk-free rate can be used)

BEVERAGE RECEIVING REPORT

In many establishments, a beverage receiving report is filled out daily by the person responsible for receiving beverages. It summarizes the invoices for all beverages received on a given day, indicates both quantities received and their values and provides columns for dividing purchases into essential categories- wines, beers, spirits and mixers- for purchase journal distribution.

HOTELS ABC
BEVERAGE RECEIVING REPORT (WEEKLY)
Week ending March 9 Date ___________

Supplier	Liqueur	Wine	Beer	Invoice Total
Atlantic Brewers			221.00	221.00
Shaw Wallace	360.00	440.00		800.00
H&G Agency		200.00		200.00
TOTALS	360.00	640.00	221.00	1221.00

CELLAR RECORDS

CELLAR INWARD BOOK

This provides accurate reference to all beverages coming into the seller and posting data for cellar mans bin cards whenever necessary it is useful to check against the perpetual beverage inventory ledger held in the food & beverage control or A/c's office.

HOTEL ABC CELLAR'S INWARD BOOK DATE............					
DATE	BEVERAGE	DELIVERY NOTE/ INVOICE NO.	BIN CARD NO	BOTTLES	HALVES
SIGNATURE OF RECEIVING OFFICER					

BIN CARDS

These are provided for each individual type of beverage & commodities held in stock and record all deliveries and issue made. The card being fixed on the shelves or racks against each beverages and commodity, showing date, quantity of goods received, quantity of goods, bin card no. referring to the same bin no. as the wine list originated from the standard bottle code list.This helps in hanling beverages and commodities.

HOTEL ABC BIN CARD BIN NO: BOTTLE SIZE TYPE: WHITE HORSE WHISKEY					
DATE	ITEMS	RECV	ISSUED TO BAR A B C	TOTAL	BALANCE

CELLAR CONTROL BOOK

This provides control of all daily deliveries to the cellar and the daily issue of each beverage from the cellar to the various bars and should cross check with the entries on the bin card and perpetual inventory, ledger held in control or accounts office.

CELLAR CONTROL BOOK

BIN CODE NO.	ITEM	UNIT	OPEN STOCK	ISSUE	TOT	RETURN	BAL STOCK	BAL BY STOCK TAKE	VARIANCE	VALUE ISS AT COST	VALUE OF BAL AT COST

BEVERAGES PERPETUAL LEDGER

This master ledger, which is prepared in control or a/c's office, consists of cards prepared for each individual type of beverages held in stock.

ULLAGE AND BREAKAGE

It is necessary for any breakage to be recorded on a standard form together with an explanation and countersigned by a member of the food and beverage department.

COMPLIMENTRY BOOK

This is necessary to record the issue of drink to the kitchen and other grades of staff as laid down by the company's policy.

EMPTY RETURN BOOK

The supplier against a delivery charges many of the containers of beverages such as crates, kegs, etc. A counter record book should be maintained, which records all container received from the various suppliers

ESTABLISHIN-G PAR STOCK

As used in bar operations, the meaning of the item par stock is somewhat different. In store room operation par stock means the maximum quantity that may be on hand at any time; it's a limit which a quantity on hand should never exceed the given quantity. In bar operations par stock is the precise quantity stated in numbers of bottles or other containers, which must be at hand on all times for each beverage at the bar.

REQUISITION SYSTEM FOR ISSUING

A requisition system is a highly structured method for issuing goods. In beverage control. A key element in the system is requisition form, on which both the beverages are issued and the quantities are recorded. No bottles should ever be issued without a written requisition signed by an authorized person.

BEVERAGE REQUISITION						
BAR DATE						
S.NO	BIN #	QTY	UNIT	ITEM	C.P UNIT TOTAL VALUE	S.P UNIT TOTAL VALUE
RECV BY REQUISITIONED BY						

K.O.T.

Kitchen Order Ticket, it is used by the waiter to give in kitchen, to take food from the kitchen, 3 copies are made, also called triplicate system.

Triplicate KOT – Structure

Logo

NAME OF ORGANISATION
NAME OF THE OUTLET

KOT NO...................

TABLE NO........... TIME............

WAITER NO............ NO. OF COVERS

QUANTITY DESCRIPTION

DATE SIGNATURE

RESTAURANT SALES SUMMARY SHEET

These are basically of all the outlet including all types of sales their charges, taxes and other required information.

Luncheon Service														Date: 23/12/2007	
Bill No.	Waiter No.	Table No.	No. of Covers	Room No.	Amount Paid: Cash	Amount Paid: Credit Card	Amount Paid: Signed	Food	Still Room Beverages	Soft Drinks	Beer and Wines	Liqueur spirit	Tobacco	Taxes	Total
031		2	4		1020			700			220			100	1020
032		5	2	305			450	250				100	50	50	450
033		11	8			4000		2500			200	300		500	4000
034		6	5	214			1150	650				350		150	1150
035		4	3			3000		1200	120	200	400	400	200	480	3000
				TOTAL	1020	7000	1600	5300	120	200	820	1650	250	1280	9620
						9620					9620				9620

RESTAURANT CHECK

This is prepared by waiter to pick up food and in case this is lost the waiter has to pay Rs. 1000 as compensation in terms of fine.

Logo & Name of the Organisation — **Bill** — No. Food/XXXX Wine/XXXX

KOT No. Room No.
Waiter No. Table No.
Name of the Outlet

Quantity	Description	Rate	Amount Rs.	Amount P.
		Total S. Charge S. Tax		
		Grand Total		

VAT No. Slogan of the Organisation

....
Cashier
E & O E

Customer's Copy

Received Rs.............................. P..... from Waiter No...............for service against KOT No............. Bill No............. at Table No................

Cashiers signature and Seal

(Cashier's copy)

Received Rs.............................. P..... from Waiter No...............for service against KOT No............. Bill No............. at Table No................

Cashiers signature and Seal

(Waiter's copy)

ACTUAL FOOD COST

Food Cost % = (Beginning Inventory + Purchases - Ending Inventory-Indirect Expenses)*100 / Food Sales. Eg.

Calculate Actual Food Cost	
Beginning inventory	10,000.00
Purchases	3,000.00
Ending inventory	10,500.00
Cost of food sold	2,500.00
Food sales	6,500.00
Actual food cost	38.46%

DAILY FOOD COST OR MONTHLY FOOD COST

Food Cost % = Food Cost * 100/Food Sales
(Where food cost = cost per item * no. of items sold
And food sales = sale price per item * no. of items sold)

Calculate Daily Or Monthly Food Cost	
Cost per item	30.00
Number of items sold	100
Total cost	3,000.00
Sales price	80.00
Number of items sold	100
Total sales	8,000.00
Potential food cost	37.50%

STATISTICAL REVENUE REPORTS

These reports directly connected to the property management system involving all the accounts nd occupancy or data records. These can be of a single property or multi property.

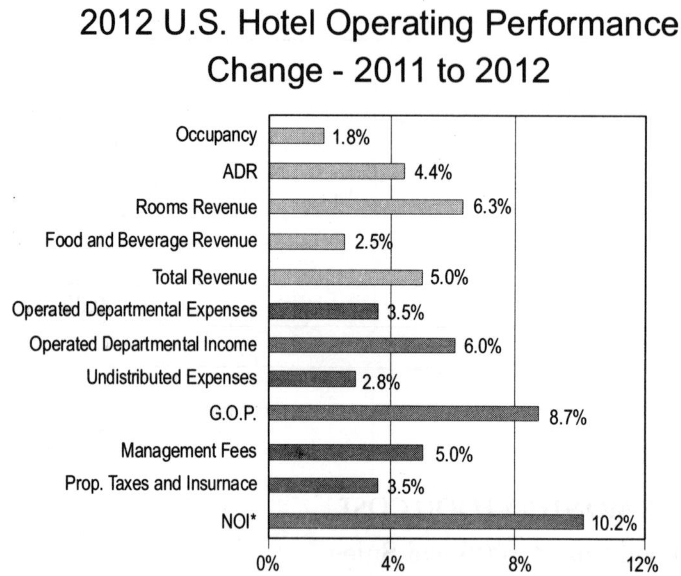

Note: *Before deductions for capital resences, rent, interest, income taxes, depreciation, and amortization
Source: PKF Hospitality Research, LLC, 2013 Trends@ in the Hotel Industry report.

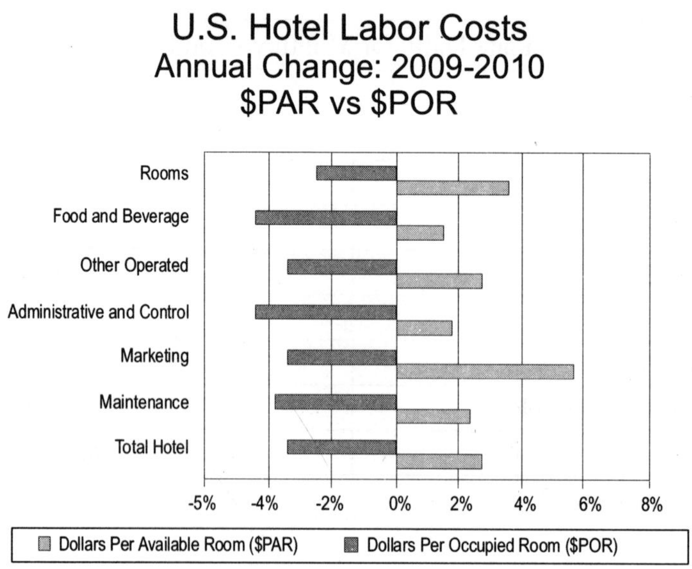

Source: PKF Hospitality Research, 2011 Trends@ in the Hotel Industry.

Occupancy and average daily rate for 2012

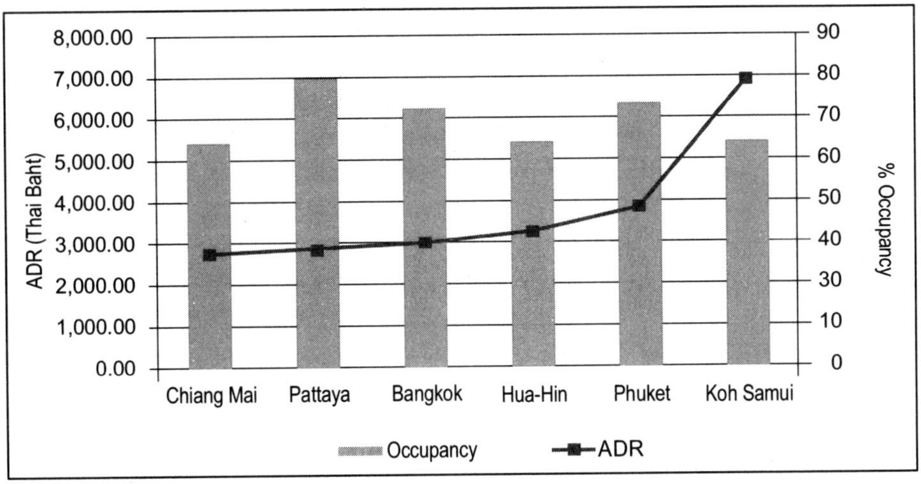

Source: STR Global

	A	B	C	D	E
1	**SOUTHWEST AIRLINES CO.**				
2	**CONSOLIDATED STATEMENT OF INCOME**				
3	**Years Ended December 31, 2010, 2009, 2008**				
4	**(In millions)**				
5		**2010**	**2009**	**2008**	
6	Operating revenues:				
7	Passenger	$11,489	$9,892	$10,549	
8	Freight	125	118	145	
9	Other	490	340	329	
10	Total operating revenues	$12,104	$10,350	$11,023	
11	Operating expenses:				
12	Salaries, wages, and benefits	$3,704	$3,468	$3,340	
13	Fuel and oil	3,620	3,044	3,713	
14	Maintenance materials and repairs	751	719	721	
15	Aircraft rentals	180	186	154	
16	Landing fees and other rentals	807	718	662	
17	Depreciation and amortization	628	616	599	
18	Other operating expenses	1,426	1,337	1,385	
19	Total operating expenses	$11,116	$10,088	$10,574	
20	Operating income	$988	$262	$449	
21	Other expenses (income):				
22	Interest expense	$167	$186	$130	
23	Capitalized interest	(18)	(21)	(25)	
24	Interest income	(12)	(13)	(26)	
25	Other (gains) losses, net	106	(54)	92	
26	Total other expenses (income)	$243	$98	$171	
27	Income before income taxes	$745	$164	$278	
28	Provision for income taxes	286	65	100	
29	Net income	$459	$99	$178	
30					
31					

CUMULATIVE AND NON-CUMULATIVE

A cumulative dividend must be paid, whereas a regular dividen d, also called a non-cumulative dividend, may be paid to or withheld from shareholders at the company's discretion. If a company cannot pay a cumulative dividend when it is due, it is still responsible for paying it in the future, possibly with interest, and it must fulfill this obligation before it can award dividends to common shareholders. This feature makes cumulative preferred shares more valuable than non-cumulative preferred shares or common shares.

CUMULATIVE SCHEME

Minimum Amount	Period (Months)	Amount Payable (Rs)	Interest p.a.	Effective Yield p.a.
Rs 10,000	12	10,800	8.00%	8.00%
	18	11,311	8.50%	8.74%
	24	11,831	9.00%	9.41%
	35	13,129	9.50%	10.43%
	48	14,377	9.50%	10.94%
	60	15,742	9.50%	11.48%

NON-CUMULATIVE SCHEME

Period (Months)	Interest p.a. (Half Yearly)	Interest p.a. (Quarterly)
12	7.75%	7.65%
24	8.75%	6.25%
36,48,60	9.25%	9.15%
Minimum Amount	Rs. 25,000	Rs. 50,000

QUESTIONNAIRE

1. What do you understand by MIS?
2. What are the different reports formed and maintained? Draw formats.
3. How is actual cost calcutaled?
4. What is daily food cost and monthly food cost?
5. Explain the statistical revenue reports with formats.
6. What is Cumulative and Non-Cumulative.
7. List the advantages of MIS?
8. Role of MIS in Hotel Industry?

GLOSSARY

1. **Acceptance Hours.** The hours of the day in which an operation is willing to accept food and beverage deliveries.
2. **Accounting Period.** A period of time, that is, hour, day, week, or month, in which an operator wishes to analyse revenue and expenses.
3. **Accounts Receivable.** The term used to refer to guest charges that have been billed to the guest but not yet collected.
4. **Actual Cost Pricing.** This method for determining menu prices is most often used by caterers. It takes the total budget amount and divides it into percentages for labour, overhead, food cost, and profit. The four percentages must equal 100 percent.
5. **Add-On Items.** Primarily used in restaurants, these are menu items that customers order in addition to their entrée such as salads, beverages, and desserts.
6. **à la carte.** Applicable to all types of food service operations, à la carte is a menu or portion of a menu on which each item is ordered separately and has its own price.
7. **Alcoholic Beverages.** Those products that are meant for consumption as a beverage and that contain a significant amount of ethyl alcohol. They are classified as beer, wine, or spirits.
8. **Apprentice.** In an apprenticeship, students work full time under a master chef and go to school part time. They are paid salaries.
9. **AP Required.** As purchased amount necessary to yield the desire EP weight. AP required is computed as EP required divided by yield percentage.
10. **As Needed.** A system of determining the purchase point by using sales forecasts and standardized recipes to decide how much of an item to place in inventory.
11. **As Purchased (AP).** This term refers to the weight or count of a product as delivered to the foodservice operator.

12. **Assembly/Serve System.** Used most commonly in cafeteria or non-restaurant settings, fully prepared foods are stored, assembled, and reheated.

13. **Attainable Food Cost.** That cost of goods consumed figure that should able given the product sales mix of a particular operation.

14. **Auditors.** Those individuals responsible for reviewing and evaluating proper operational procedures.

15. **Average.** The value arrived at by adding the quantities in a series and dividing the sum of the quantities by the number of items in the series.

16. **Average Sales Per Guest.** The mean amount of money spent per customer during a given financial accounting period. Often referred to as check average.

17. **Bill Of Lading.** Document that conveys title to the goods purchased.

18. **Back Of The House.** The kitchen production area of a foodservice establishment.

19. **Back Haul.** Occurs when a driver delivers a shipment to a hospitality operation and then refills the empty truck with items that needed to be delivered to another location.

20. **Bain-Marie.** A kitchen term that can refer to a hot water bath or the vessel used for the hot water bath. The hot water bath is used to keep foods hot.

21. **Banquet Cart.** This mobile piece of equipment is typically used for buffet-style dining. This cart may be insulated or non-insulated and typically comes equipped with shelving or racks for plates, and an electrically powered heating or refrigeration device.

22. **Bars and Taverns.** Considered a category of the food services industry, the United States Census Bureau defines them as establishments known as bars, taverns, night clubs, or drinking places primarily engaged in preparing and serving alcoholic beverages for immediate consumption.

23. **Beer.** A fermented beverage made from grain and flavoured with hops.

24. **Beer System.** A method used in some restaurants or bars for beer dispensing. The kegs of beers are kept in a refrigerated location and a system of pressurized, insulated, and refrigerated lines transports it to dispensers at the bar.

25. **Beginning Inventory.** The dollar value of all products on hand at the beginning of the accounting period. This amount is determined by completing a physical inventory.
26. **Best Price.** The lowest price that meets the requirement of both the food service operation and its vendor.
27. **Beverage Costs.** The costs related to the sale of alcoholic beverages.
28. **Bid Sheet.** A form used to compare prices among many vendors in order to select the best prices.
29. **Bin Card.** An index card with both additions to and deletions from inventory of a given product. To facilitate its use, the card is usually affixed to the shelf that holds the given item. Used in a perpetual inventory system.
30. **Biological Hazard.** Not just a medical term, in the food services industry this term refers to the potential contamination of food by pathogenic microorganisms.
31. **Bonding.** Purchasing an insurance policy to protect the operation in case of employee theft.
32. **Branded Product Costs.** An accounting term for franchisees, this refers to the costs of products it is necessary to buy to maintain the franchise or license agreement.
33. **Break-Even Point.** The point at which operational expenses are exactly equal to sales revenue.
34. **Broken Case.** A case of beverage products in which several different brands or products make up the contents of the case.
35. **Broker.** A wholesaler who brings buyers and sellers together.
36. **Budget.** A forecast or estimate of projected revenue, expense, and profit for a defined accounting period. Often referred to as plan.
37. **Blind Receiving.** When the invoice accompanying a delivery contains only the names of the items delivered. Quantity and price information is missing.
38. **Blast Chillers.** A refrigeration unit that circulates cold air. The benefit to using it is that it can reduce the temperatures of hot foods very quickly.
39. **Brix.** A kitchen term that refers to the percentage of sugar in a product that contains syrup or other sugar solution.

40. **Bundling.** The practice of selecting specific menu items and pricing them as a group, in such a manner that the single menu price of the group is lower than if the items comprising the group were purchased individually.

41. **Business and Industry.** This is a segment of the food services industry that feeds employees in offices, factories, and plants.

42. **Buying Groups.** Companies that consolidate purchases and provide support for their distributor members.

43. **Call-In.** A system whereby employees who are off duty are required to check in with management on a daily basis to see if the volume is such that they may be needed.

44. **Call Liquors.** Those spirits that are requested (called for) by a particular brand name.

45. **Carryover.** A menu item prepared for sale during a meal period but carried over for use in a different meal period.

46. **Category Food Cost Percentage.** A food cost percentage computed on a portion of total food usage. Categories include meat, seafood, dairy, produce, etc.

47. **Cherry Picker.** A customer who buys only those items from a supplier that are the lowest in price among the supplier's competition.

48. **Check Averages.** Used as a measurement and defining factor most often in the food services industry, this term refers to the average dollar amount of checks at a particular restaurant.

49. **COLA.** Cost of living adjustment. A term to describe a raise in employee pay.

50. **Comp.** Short for the word complimentary, which refers to the practice of management giving a product to a guest without a charge. This can be done fora special customer or as a way of making amends for an operational error.

51. **Comfort Foods.** Menu items intended to remind customers of old fashioned, traditional, home-cooked American meals.

52. **Commercial Establishments.** In the industry this term refers to public establishments, which could be housed in freestanding buildings or included in or part of another establishment

53. **Commissary System.** Used primarily by food service operations with

multiple locations, a central production kitchen controls the cooking and food supply and delivers the food to the other location.

54. **Contract Price.** A price mutually agreed upon by supplier and operator. This price is the amount to be paid for a product or products over a prescribed period of time.

55. **Contribution Margin.** The profit or margin that remains after product cost is subtracted from an item's selling price.

56. **Contribution Margin For Overall Operation.** The dollar amount that contributes to covering fixed costs and providing for a profit.

57. **Contract Food Services.** Used most commonly by non-restaurant operations, this refers to companies that offer cafeteria or food services to their employees, but have contracted with outside vendors to supply the food and/or service.

58. **Contribution Margin Income Statement.** A financial summary that shows P&L items in terms of sales, variable costs, contribution margin, fixed costs, and profit.

59. **Contribution Margin Per Menu Item.** The amount that remains after the product cost of the menu item is subtracted from the item's selling price.

60. **Controllable Expense.** An expense in which the decisions made by the food service manager can have the effect of either increasing or reducing the expense.

61. **Cost Of Food Consumed.** The actual dollar value of all food used, or consumed, by the operation.

62. **Cost Of Food Sold.** The dollar amount of all food actually sold, thrown away, wasted, or stolen plus or minus transfers from other units, minus employee meals.

63. **Costing.** An important part of budgeting, forecasting, and planning, this is the process used to determine an operation's costs and potential profits.

64. **Critical Control Point.** Part of the HACCP food safety process, any point in a food system where loss of control could pose an unacceptable health risk.

65. **Cost Per Guest.** A method of analyzing costs that uses the total expense and total number of guests served to establish an actual cost of servicing each guest.

66. **Count.** Term used to designate size.

67. **Credit Memo.** An addendum to the vendor's delivery slip (invoice) that reconciles differences between the delivery slip and the purchase order.

68. **Cycle Menu.** A menu that is in effect for a predetermined length of time such as7 days or 14 days.

69. **Daily Inventory Sheet.** A form that lists the items in storage, the unit of purchase, and the par value. It also contains the following columns: on hand, special order, and order amount.

70. **Daily Menu.** A menu that changes every day.

71. **Desired Profit.** The profit that an owner seeks to achieve on a predicted quantity of revenue.

72. **Draft Beer.** The term used to identify beer products sold in a keg.

73. **ECR.** Electronic cash registers that also maintain data of all products sold.

74. **Edible Portion.** This is a kitchen term that refers to the weight of a menu item after it has been trimmed, prepared, and cooked.

75. **Danger Zone.** In the food services industry this term refers to the United States Food and Drug Administration's determination that foods at temperatures between 41 and 140 degrees are at higher risk for contamination.

76. **Delivery Ticket.** Written receipt summarizing what was ordered and delivered.

77. **Dram Shop Laws.** The term used to describe a series of legislative acts that, under certain conditions, holds businesses and, in some cases, individuals, personally responsible for the actions of guests who consume excessive amounts of alcoholic beverages. These "laws" shift the liability for acts committed by an individual under the influence of alcohol from that individual to the server or operation that supplied the intoxicating beverage.

78. **Edible Portion (EP).** This term refers to the weight or count of a product after it has been trimmed, cooked, and portioned.

79. **Embezzlement.** The term used to describe theft of a type where the money, although legally possessed by the embezzler, is diverted to the embezzler by his or her fraudulent action.

80. **Ending Inventory.** The dollar value of all products on hand at the end of the accounting period. This amount is determined by completing a physical inventory.

81. **Ethics.** The choices of proper conduct made by an individual in his or her relationships with others.

82. **Expense.** The price paid to obtain the items required to operate the business. Often referred to as cost.

83. **Extended Price.** The price per unit multiplied by the number of units. This refers to a total unit price on a delivery slip or invoice.

84. **FIFO.** With the first-in, first-out method of storage, the operator intends to sell his or her oldest product before selling the most recently delivered product.

85. **Fiscal Year.** Start and stop dates for a 365-day accounting period. This period need not begin in January and end in December.

86. **Fixed Average.** The average amount of sales or volume over a specific series or time period, for example, first month of the year or second week of the second month.

87. **Fixed Expense.** An expense that remains constant despite increases or decreases in sales volume.

88. **Fixed Payroll.** Those dollars spent on employees such as managers, receiving clerks, and dieticians whose presence is not generally directly dependent on the number of guests served.

89. **First-In-First-Out.** Used by a variety of food services organizations, this is a food inventory method that is used to ensure that products are used in the order they arrive at the location.

90. **Forecasting.** The estimate of the quantity of food needed for a day or other specified time period.

91. **Food Cost Percentage.** The portion of food sales that was spent on food expenses.

92. **Food Costs.** The dollar costs associated with actually producing the menu item(s) a guest selects.

93. **Forecasting.** The process of estimating future revenue or expenses of a hospitality operation.

94. **Franchiser.** The entity responsible for selling and maintaining control over the franchise name. (Alternative spelling: franchisor.)

95. **Free-Pouring.** Pouring liquor from a bottle without measuring the poured amount.

96. **Fresh Dated.** A food package upon which a date is stamped to indicate the freshness of its contents.

97. **Full-Service Restaurants.** Restaurants that offer a relatively broad menu along with table, counter, and/or booth service. Customers are waited on at their tables rather than walking to order counter.

98. **Goal Value Analysis.** A menu pricing and analysis system that compares goals of the foodservice operation to performance of individual menu items.

99. **Goods Available For Sale.** The sum of the beginning inventory and purchases. It represents the value of all food that was available for sale during the accounting period.

100. **Grade.** In the food services industry meats, poultry, and eggs are given grades to designate their quality. The higher the quality of the product, the higher the grade will be.

101. **Gross Margin.** Accounting term that indicates the amount derived by subtracting the unit cost from the unit price, or total cost from total price.

102. **Gross-Profit Pricing.** This method of menu pricing is appropriate for established organizations with several months of history, and after an item has been on the menu prior to knowing its actual costs. This is calculated using the following information: past revenue in dollars, past gross profit in dollars, past number of customers, and the item's actual food cost.

103. **Group Purchasing Organizations.** Organizations of the food services industry whose main function is to consolidate purchases and provide support for their food service distributor members. Most small, medium, and even some large broad line distributors are members of a group purchasing organization.

104. **Guest Check.** A written record of what was purchased by the guest and how much the guest was charged for the item(s).

105. **Guest Count.** The number of individuals served in a defined time period.

106. **Half-Bottle.** A bottle of wine that is approximately one-half the size of the standard750-ml wine bottle. Typically sold for either room service or dining room consumption. Also known as a split.

107. **Hardware.** The machines and equipment used to operate computer software.

108. **Hazard Analysis.** Used in all food service operations, this is a system for food safety that details safe food handling procedures and potential hazards to food safety.

109. **Head Size.** The amount of space on the top of a glass of beer that is made up off o am. Thus, a glass of beer with 1 inch of foam on its top is said to have a1-inch head.

110. **House Wine.** The term used to indicate the type of wine to be served in the event a specific brand name product is not requested by the guest.

111. **Hydrometer.** An instrument used to measure the specific gravity of a liquid.

112. **Ideal Expense.** Management's view of the correct or appropriate amount of expense necessary to generate a given quantity of sales.

113. **Ingredient Room.** A storeroom or section of a storeroom where ingredients are weighed and measured according to standardized recipes and then delivered to the appropriate kitchen production area.

114. **Inventory Turnover.** The number of times the total value of inventory has been purchased and replaced in an accounting period. Storage by management for use in an operation.

115. **In-house Management**. Mainly used in food service operations other than restaurants, this term primarily refers to facilities that own and operate their own food service departments.

116. **Invoice Receiving.** Common type of receiving procedure. Involves comparing the invoice with the order record and then proceeding to check quality, quantity, and AP prices of items delivered.

117. **Invoice.** A bill from a vendor for goods or services, often presented as the goods are delivered or after the services performed.

118. **K-Minus.** Industry term used to refer to a food service facility that does not contain a kitchen. Instead a central kitchen prepares the food and transports it to the facility.

119. **Jigger.** A bar device used to measure predetermined quantities of alcoholic beverages. Jiggers usually are marked in ounces and portions of an ounce, for example, 1 ounce or 11D 2 ounces.

120. **Job Description.** A listing of the tasks to be performed in a particular position.

121. **Job Specification.** A listing of the personal skills and characteristics needed to perform those tasks pertaining to a particular job description.

122. **Layout.** Used primarily in kitchens, this refers to a plan for equipment placement in a given room.

123. **Labour Expense.** All expenses (costs), including payroll, required to maintain a work force in a foodservice operation.

124. **LIFO.** With the last-in, first-out method of storage, the operator intends to sell his or her most recently delivered product before selling the older product.

125. **Loss Leader.** A menu item that is priced very low for the purpose of drawing Large numbers of customers to the operation.

126. **Managerial Accounting.** The process of documenting and analyzing sales, expenses, and profits. Sometimes referred to as cost accounting.

127. **Minimum Order Requirement.** The smallest order, usually expressed in dollar value, that can be placed with a vendor who delivers.

128. **Minimum Sales Point (MSP).** The dollar sales volume required to justify staying open.

129. **Minimum Staff.** The term used to designate the least number of employees, or payroll dollars, required to operate a facility or department within the facility.

130. **Mixed Expense.** An expense that has properties of both a fixed and a variable expense.

131. **Meat Tag.** It contains two parts duplicate parts. One part is attached to the item when it is received and placed into storage, the other one goes into the controller's office.

132. **Menu Explosion.** Used by management or owners to determine kitchen equipment needs in new or remodel kitchens, this is a process that calculates the amounts of food prepared for each menu item in a specific kitchen.

133. **Menu Matrix.** A menu matrix is used to determine the amount of products sold in a restaurant, and is typically used to determine food costs.

134. **Menu Pattern or Meal Plan.** This term can be used by all categories of

the food services industry and refers to an outline of each menu category and the number of selections offered in each category.

135. **Negligent Hiring.** Failure on the part of an employer to exercise reasonable care in the selection of employees.

136. **Net Income.** The profit realized after all expenses and appropriate taxes for a business have been paid.

137. **Night Drop.** When the delivery driver has a key to the facility, enters it when closed for business, leaves the shipment, locks up, and goes.

138. **Non-Controllable Expense.** An expense that the foodservice manager can neither increase nor decrease.

139. **Occupancy Costs.** Expenses related to occupying and paying for the physical facility that houses the foodservice unit.

140. **OJT.** On-the-job training. A method of training in which workers are training while they actually are performing their required tasks.

141. **On-Call.** A system whereby selected employees who are off duty can be contacted by management on short notice to cover for other employees who are absent or to come to work if customer demand suddenly increases.

142. **Open Bar.** A bar in which no charge for an individual drink is made to the customer, thus establishing an all-you-can-drink environment. Sometimes refer red to as a hotel bar.

143. **Opportunity Cost.** The cost of foregoing the next best alternative when making a decision. For example, with two choices, A & B, both having potential benefits or returns, if A is chosen, then the potential benefits from choosing Bare lost.

144. **Other Expenses.** The expenses of an operation that are neither food, beverage, nor labour.

145. **Oxidation.** A process that occurs when oxygen comes in contact with bottled wine, resulting in a deterioration of the wine product.

146. **Padded Inventory.** The term used to describe the inappropriate activity of adding a value for non-existing inventory items to the value of total inventory in an effort to understate actual costs.

147. **Par Level.** A system of determining the purchase point by using management established minimum and maximum allowable inventory levels for a given inventory item.

148. **Payroll.** Total wages and salaries paid by a foodservice operation to its employees.

149. **Percent.** The number "out of each hundred." Thus, 10 percent means 10 out of each 100. This is computed by dividing the part by the whole.

150. **Percent Selecting.** A formula for determining the proportion of people will buy a given menu item from a list of menu choices.

151. **Percentage Variance.** The change in sales, expressed as a percentage that results from comparing two operating periods.

152. **Perpetual Inventory.** An inventory control system in which additions to and deletions from total inventory are noted as they occur.

153. **Perpetual Inventory Card.** A bin card that includes the product's price at the top of the card, allowing for continual tracking of the quantity of an item on hand and its price.

154. **Physical Inventory.** An inventory control system in which an actual or physical count and valuation of all inventory on hand is taken at the close of each accounting period.

155. **Physical Inventory.** An actual counting and valuing of all products kept in your hospitality operation.

156. **Point Of Sales (POS) System.** A system for controlling hospitality operations' cash and product usage by using a computer processor depending on the size of the operation, additional computer hardware communication devices, and/or software.

157. **Popularity Index.** The percentage of total guests choosing a given menu item from a list of menu alternatives.

158. **Predicted Number To Be Sold.** A method of determining the number of a given menu item that is likely to be sold if the total number of customers to be served is known.

159. **Premium Liquors.** Expensive call liquors.

160. **Price Blending.** The process of assigning prices based on product groups for the purpose of achieving predetermined cost objectives.

161. **Price Spread.** The difference in price on a menu between the lowest and highest priced item of a similar nature.

162. **Productivity.** The amount of work performed by a worker in a set amount of time.

163. **Productivity Ratio.** This formula refers to the total unit output divided by the total unit input.

164. **Productivity Standard.** Management's expectation of the productivity ratio of each employee. Also, management's view of what constitutes the appropriate productivity ratio in a given foodservice unit or units.

165. **Product Specification.** A detailed description of an ingredient or menu item.

166. **Pilferage.** Refers to minor theft. For instance, employees snatching a drink while on the clock, or guests swiping a wine glass.

167. **Profit.** The dollars that remain after all expenses have been paid. Often referred to as net income.

168. **Profit and Loss Statement (P&L).** A detailed listing of revenue and expenses fora given accounting period.

169. **Projected Sales.** Sales that may be determined by either dollar sales or customer count. Projected sales are established by using sales histories and other knowledge the operator may have that could impact total volume. They are predictions of future sales volume.

170. **Pull Date.** Expiration date on beverage products, usually beers, after which they should not be sold.

171. **Purchase Order.** A listing of products requested by the purchasing agent. The purchase order, or PO, lists various product information, including quantity ordered and price quoted by the vendor.

172. **Purchase Point.** The point in time when an item held in inventory reaches a level that indicates it should be reordered.

173. **Purchases.** The sum cost of all food purchased during the accounting period. Determined by adding all properly tabulated invoices for the accounting period.

174. **Quick-Change Artist.** A guest who, having practiced the routine many times, attempts to confuse the cashier; in his or her confusion, the cashier gives the guest too much change.

175. **Recipe Ready.** A recipe ingredient that is cleaned, trimmed, cooked, and generally completed, save for its addition to the recipe.

176. **Refusal Hours.** Those hours of the day in which an operation refuses to accept food and beverage deliveries.

177. **Reporting Period.** The process of reporting a time period for which records are being maintained. This may be of the same duration as an accounting period.

178. **Requisition.** When a food or beverage product is requested from storage by an employee for use in an operation.

179. **Return On Sales (ROS).** Often referred to as operating profit percentage. RO Scan also be stated in whole dollar terms.

180. **Revenue.** The term used to indicate the dollars taken in by the business in a defined period of time. Often referred to as sales.

181. **Rolling Average.** The average amount of sales or volume over a changing time period, for example, the last ten days or the last three weeks.

182. **Stock Requisition.** A formal request made by an employee for items needed to carry out necessary tasks.

183. **Safety Stock.** These are additions to par stock, held as a hedge against the possibility of extra demand for a given product. This helps reduce the risk of being out of stock on a given item.

184. **Salaried Employee.** An employee who receives the same income per week or month regardless of the number of hours worked.

185. **Sales Forecast.** A prediction of the number of guests to be served and the revenues they will generate in a defined, future time period.

186. **Sales History.** A record of sales achieved by an operator in a given sales outlet during a specifically identified time period.

187. **Sales Mix.** The series of consumer purchasing decisions that result in a specific food and beverage cost percentage. Sales mix affects overall product cost percentage any time menu items have varying food beverage cost percentages.

188. **Sales to Date.** The cumulative sales figures reported during a given financial accounting period.

189. **Sales Variance.** An increase or decrease from previously experienced or predicted sales levels.

190. **Sales Volume.** The number of units sold.

191. **Spoilage.** Deterioration of food by microbial or chemical action.

192. **Storage Space.** The amount of room, for example, the number of cubic feet, devoted to storeroom and warehouse facilities.

193. **Separated.** The term used to describe employees who have either quit, been terminated, or in some other manner have left their place of employment.

194. **Shelf Life.** The period of time an ingredient or menu item maintains its freshness, flavour, and quality.

195. **Shorting.** When the vendor is unable to deliver the quantity of item ordered for the appointed delivery date.

196. **Software.** The set of instructions that control the workings of computer hardware and direct the processing of data.

197. **SOP.** Acronym for standard operating procedure.

198. **Slacked Out.** A food item that is thought to be fresh but has actually been frozen, thawed, and passed off as fresh.

199. **Source Reduction.** Working with food manufacturers and wholesalers to reduce product packaging waste.

200. **Spirits.** Fermented beverages that are distilled to increase the alcohol content of the product.

201. **Split Shift.** A scheduling technique used to match individual employee work shifts with the peaks and valleys of customer demand.

202. **Spotter.** An individual employed by management for the purpose of inconspicuously observing bartenders and wait staff in order to detect a fraudulent or policy violating behaviour.

203. **Standard Cost.** The labour cost needed to meet established productivity standards.

204. **Standardized Recipe.** The procedures to be used for consistently preparing and serving a given menu item

205. **Standardized Recipe Cost Sheet.** A record of the ingredient costs required to produce an item sold by a foodservice operation.

206. **Standard Menu.** A printed and otherwise fixed menu that stays the same day after day.

207. **Task Training.** The training undertaken to ensure an employee has the skills to meet productivity goals.

208. **Two-Key System.** A system to control access to storage areas.

209. **Transfer Slip.** Document used to control and account for products moved from one unit to another one within the same company.

210. **Uniform Systems Of Accounts.** Standardized sets of procedures used for categorizing revenue and expense in a defined industry, for example, uniform system of accounts for restaurants (USAR).

211. **Value Pricing.** The practice of reducing all or most prices on the menu the belief that total guest counts will increase to the point that total sales revenue also increases.

212. **Variable Expense.** An expense that generally increases as sales volume increases and decreases as sales volume decreases.

213. **Variable Payroll.** Those dollars expended on employees whose presence is directly dependent on the number of guests served. These employees include servers, bartenders, and dishwashers, for example. As the number of guests served increases, the number of these individuals required to do the job also increases. As the number of guests served decreases, variable payroll should decrease.

214. **Vintage.** The specific year(s) of production for a wine.

215. **Vintner.** Wine producer.

■